ON STAGE!
Short Plays for Acting Students

BY ROBERT MAURO

MERIWETHER PUBLISHING LTD.
Colorado Springs, Colorado

Meriwether Publishing Ltd., Publisher
P.O. Box 7710
Colorado Springs, CO 80933

Book Design: Tom Myers
Executive Editor: Arthur L. Zapel
Typography: Sharon E. Garlock

© Copyright MCMXC Meriwether Publishing Ltd.
Printed in the United States of America
First Edition

Library of Congress Cataloging-in-Publication Data

On stage! : short plays for acting students / [edited] by Robert
    Mauro. — 1st ed.
            p.   cm.
        ISBN 0-916260-67-4
        1. Acting.   2. Monologues.   3. Dialogues.   I. Mauro, Robert,
    1946-
    PN2080.05   1990
    822'.04108--dc20   90-52982
                                                                      CIP

DEDICATION

For all my friends.
You know who you are,
and I'm glad I know you.
For Arthur L. Zapel,
a good and fair critic;
for Murray Kerner,
my eighth grade teacher,
who opened my eyes to the written word;
for New York City's Mayor
Fiorello LaGuardia,
who, in the days after the Great Depression,
gave my dad, then a poor high school graduate,
an old Underwood typewriter which
Dad used to get his first job, and which,
as a child,
I wrote my first stories on.
For my parents,
who never criticized my spelling,
and always laughed at my stories.
But most of all,
for Marli,
whom I'll love from sunrise to sunset
for what she has given me:
a good ear, a good heart,
and endless love.

PREFACE

The short play is a wonderful medium for the actor and the director. It gives them the opportunity to communicate an idea and to make the audience laugh and cry, think and feel, all in a brief moment of time. The short play has the power to hold the audience's attention and focus it on one particular incident by using dialog, situation, costume, lighting, sound, and the unexpected. The short play's very brevity would seem to suggest it is simplistic, but it is not. It is no different from the three-act play in that it has a beginning, a middle and an end — and the potential to move an audience — to make it think. It does this through its actors and its director, and its playwright — all of whom work together, using plot, conflict, characterization, and dialog. These things, and the actors' and director's ability, are what make the characters real, unique individuals, each with his or her own life and personality. A good director, good actors, and a good playwright can magically transform the written word into real life ON STAGE!

The short play ideally focuses on one incident in time. Where is this all happening? In an office, an elevator, at home, in a park? Wherever the action takes place, in a short play, it's a good idea to stick to one set, one situation. Nothing that is not absolutely necessary to the plot should be there. Scenery, costumes, every character must have a good reason to exist. And that is what I have tried to do in these short plays. Scenery costs money, costumes cost money, and actors cost money, or must be available, and the less costly a play is to produce, the greater the chances it will have of being seen.

Now that you know the basic ingredients that go into producing a good short play, it's time to go ON STAGE! And when you do, if you have brought everything together in just the right way, you may end up with something that an audience might just remember, be entertained by, and, it is hoped, learn from. And if you can do that, you can feel good no matter what happens when the curtain finally comes down. Not only on any one of these short one-act plays, but on the bigger drama of life.

TABLE OF CONTENTS

MONOLOGS

DUOLOGS

COMEDY SKETCHES

LIGHT DRAMA

SERIOUS DRAMA

MONOLOGS

The Paper Boy

PRODUCTION NOTES

PLAYER: 1 male.

PLAYING TIME: About 10 minutes. (Adjustable with edits.)

COSTUME: Period clothes, baseball cap.

PROPERTIES: Newspapers, old bicycle.

The Paper Boy

CHARACTER: DANNY, town newspaper boy.

TIME: Daybreak, long ago.

SETTING: DANNY stands beside his old bicycle in town square. There is a flagpole with flag and sign that says FUTURE SITE OF MIDDLEBURY GROVE WAR MEMORIAL.

AT RISE: DANNY is folding his newspapers, getting them ready for delivery.

DANNY: *(Looks up.)* **Oh, hi. My name's Danny. I'm the town newspaper boy. I'm here in our town's square,** *(Points to sign)* **the future site of our Middlebury Grove War Memorial. She's going to be a beauty, I hear. Anyhow, as I said, I'm the town paper boy. I just picked up my papers at Mr. Anderson's General Store.**

Mr. Anderson's store is right next to the brand new Food-o-rama. You can get any kind of food there in a minute or two. Very modern. Very fast.

Anyhow, it's Saturday morning and I have my weekly papers to deliver. It's a great job being a paper boy. You get to make a little money and you get to meet a lot of interesting people. Old and young; married and single. And I deliver to them all.

Mr. Ross, the publisher, even lets me write a little story now and then. My dad is an editor on the newspaper. I like to write. I write little plays now in fact for my friends. Mom helps make the scenery out of her old drapes and things.

Maybe someday I'll be a writer. I'll write all about something. Maybe something about our town. But right now I'm just a paper boy. And I have a bunch of papers to deliver. Before I do, though, I'm here just folding them all so I can toss them from my bike. I can toss a paper

farther than any paper boy I know. Of course, I don't know any but me. We are a small town. *(Pause)*

I've been told I have a great arm, which is why I'm a pitcher on our town's little league team. But on Saturday mornings, I'm a paper boy. I've been delivering these newspapers in town for quite a while now. We have a nice town here. Everyone knows everyone else. It never seems to change. But it does, I guess.

The state just built a brand new turn-off on the State Road. With it came that brand new Food-o-rama. The fastest food in the West, the sign up front says. They even have a big ad in the newspaper. Yep. A good place to eat if you're in a hurry. Had my breakfast there this morning, in fact. Do every Saturday morning now. Lets Mom sleep late. She doesn't have to fix my breakfast anymore. Sort of miss that, but that's progress, I suppose. And the folks at the Food-o-rama are real nice. Like me, they get up real early — even earlier than I do.

We're all good workers here in Middlebury Grove. Most of us work. Most folks like it. I like it, too. Yeah.

We're getting a new generator, too, for Mr. Edison's electric light. And even a new phone operator. And something called a motel is being built right off the new State Road exit. I might even get a few more customers to deliver my newspapers to. I hear they're going to be building a few new homes. Imagine that! A Sears Roebuck could be next. You never know. Mr. Anderson, who owns the general store, won't like that. It's hard to compete with those big city chain stores, but that's progress. We're moving into the modern age, the modern world. Well, it's about time. *(Pause)*

We don't have much hoopla here in Middlebury Grove. There's the Founder's Day Parade in the summer. In the winter, we settle for a big Christmas tree every Christmas down here in the town square and a full set of electric Chanukah candles. And there is the new war memorial. *(He stands and points to indicate points of interest as he talks.)* You'd probably like to visit our little town, but knowing most folks, you probably wouldn't want to live here. You'd miss your big city subway system and those big department stores. We do have a department store here in town — well, sort of. Tell you about it in a minute.

But first let me draw you a sort of mental map of where I live. *(Points east)* To the east, we have our school — kindergarten to high school. Reverend Radcliff's church is over beyond the school. Then comes the firehouse. We just got a new horseless fire engine. Mr. O'Connor, our fire chief, likes it. Molly, our fire horse, isn't quite sure. *(Walks to east a bit.)* Then farther east there's our post office farther up the street — Main Street. To the west we have a dance palace, strictly for the family — the whole family. After the dance palace comes the bank, a general store and two gas stations and one library.

We don't have a hospital and Doc Fredricks is pretty old, so if you get real sick, it's eighty miles down the State Road to our nearest hospital. Yes, they take all sorts of folks, rich and poor and in between. So does old Doc Fredricks. Oh, yeah. You got a sick horse? See old Doc Fredricks. Old Doc Fred is also our local veterinarian. Don't panic. He's a real MD, a people doctor, but he fixes our horses, cats and dogs, too.

But back to our gas stations. We have a lot of those new tin lizzies passing by up and down the State Road. And trucks delivering oranges, milk and food and such. So both gas stations are also truck stops. One Mr. Johnson owns, and he makes sausage and eggs and burgers for the truckers. Miss Peters owns the other gas station. She took it over when her daddy died. She makes pot roast, sandwiches, apple pie and dumplings. I love her dumplings. Yeah. Miss Peters is OK. She's a great cook and real good with automobiles and trucks. Fixes Mr. Wilkerson's all the time.

Mr. W's the town banker and richest citizen. He helped buy the new fire engine. When we have a fire, every man that can comes to help put out the fires. But Mr. Wilkerson always insists on doing the driving. But back to gas stations. Now Mr. Johnson, he's not so good with autos. But he's real good at sausage and eggs and burgers — and fixing bicycles. He fixed mine twice this month alone. I put a lot of miles on it delivering my papers.

Anyway, to the north we have the . . . er . . . the *(Smiles)* department store — if you can call it that. Actually, it's a bunch of stores — you know — clothes, lumber, toys, hobbies, sporting goods and ice cream parlor. The store owners saw the department stores in the big city magazines, so they hired Harvey Stoner, our town architect, and had Mr. Stoner construct a covered walkway so you won't get wet when it rains. He did an excellent job. People now shop — come rain, hail, snow, or sleet.

Of course, my mom always did shop regardless of the weather and probably always will. She's good at it, too. Knows a bargain when she sees one. So does my dad.

Dad is still saying when everyone has electric lights, we'll have 'em too. For now gas is good enough. He likes coal heat, too. Oil is too modern for Dad. Gramps used to say that, too. He was a minister. And Grandma hated electric lights. Said they hurt her eyes. She preferred candles herself. Anyhow, Mr. Stoner designed and built the covered walkway — or department store, if you will.

He's now working on *(Points to sign)* our town's future war memorial. It's going to be a small memorial. We aren't a wealthy town. And we only had two town residents die in the war. Both heroes. There was Bill Douglas and Charlie Truette. Both died when the battleship Maine was blown up. It was all over the papers. Big headlines even here, but that was before my time. Most wars were. *(Points to backdrop.)*

To the south, we have our police department. We have one policeman. Officer O'Mally. He arrested someone once, but no one can remember who. Way back, behind the police station, is our ball field. My team nearly won the county title there two summers ago. I pitched. *(Pause)*

Beyond the field is the woods where some of us hunt, and beyond the woods is the big pond where most of us fish. I caught a bass up there one year. He was this big. *(Measures out two feet with his hands.)* Well . . . maybe this big. *(Measures out a foot or so.)* Felt like a monster though when I hooked him. *(Looks around.)*

So there you have it. My home town, Middlebury Grove. I've told you about most of it — well, our little city's business district and non-residential section anyway. By the way, *(Points to self)* I call this here place a town, but the local politicians and the town fathers insist on calling our little town a city. Something to do with property values or the state capital, I guess. *(Shrugs)* Or taxes. Are taxes higher in a city or in a town? *(Shrugs)* Beats me. Anyway, city does sound more impressive than town — at least, I guess, if you're a town politician. *(Folds rest of papers and begins to pile them into his bike's basket.)*

By the way, I just picked these up at our local general store over on Main Street. And now, as I said, I'm folding them here in the town square. You get to hear the birds singing in the morning, and you even get to witness a great view of the sun coming up over Reverend Radcliff's Episcopal church steeple, where I sing in the choir. *(Folds more papers, then:)* **It's like that every Saturday morning. And like every Saturday morning, I have a few deliveries in town, then I head west past our dance palace, bank, general store, and our two gas stations. Then I'm in the country.**

We have farms and a few small clusters of houses. I deliver to all sorts of people. Like Mr. Appleton, our postman. I get to see a lot of friendly folks. For instance, there's old Miss Biddle. She's got to be nearly a hundred now. She's been real old ever since I can remember. She never married. Always was independent. Talks on and on about the vote for women. Says someday they'll have it too. My mom says, "Why?" Oh, Mom knows. My mom is very smart. *(Thinks)* **You think women will have the vote?** *(Shrugs)* **I don't know. But Miss Biddle sure thinks it's important, and she should know. She's a pretty smart lady. She now lives alone on her parents' farm. Miss Biddle is pretty lively for nearly a hundred. She always has cookies and milk for me.** *(Looks down for a second, then:)* **I'm not crazy about her cookies. I think she forgot the recipe. I tell her I'll eat them along the way, you know, after a hard day of delivering papers, when I get hungry. But actually, I feed them to the birds. The birds seem to like them. Don't tell Miss Biddle I do that! Please! I wouldn't want to hurt her feelings. She's really nice. But I once tasted one of her cookies.** *(Makes a little face.)* **Maybe she makes them with bird seed instead of flour. She is always feeding the birds.** *(Scratches his head.)* **I don't know. But don't ask me to eat them. I get this feeling I'll end up on the obituary page of** *(Holds up a newspaper)* **our paper if I do.** *(Pause)* **Yeah, she's something, old Miss Biddle.**

I hear when she was younger she was a teacher right here at our school. They say she went to a college up in New England. An all-girl's college. She then came back home and taught in our school for nearly sixty years. She

started teaching at the high school level and ended her career teaching the little kids in kindergarten. Now she makes me milk and cookies. She makes everyone milk and cookies. And she loves to talk. Never seems to want to see me go. Not many people ever go out to see old Miss Biddle, except Reverend Radcliff. He always leaves with a big box of cookies. I wonder if he feeds them to the birds, or maybe the pigeons in the church yard. *(Pauses to fold a few papers.)*

We have one church in town. Episcopal. We share it with the Catholics, the Methodists, and our Jewish town folk. There's room for everyone at Reverend Radcliff's church. I guess when Miss Biddle finally dies, she'll be buried in our church cemetery. Everyone else is. *(Pause)*

After I deliver to Miss Biddle, I deliver to the Davidsons, our newest town residents. Mr. Davidson is a writer from the big city. He bought the old Maxwell farm so he and Mrs. Davidson could get away from the hustle and bustle of the big city. Mr. Davidson occasionally writes articles for *(Holds up paper)* our paper. So does his wife. Yeah. She's a writer, too. Novels, Gothics. Like Hawthorne. Two of them already. My mom says I'm too young to read them yet. But I can read anything Mr. Davidson writes. Yeah, sure, because Mr. Davidson writes children's books. Maybe you heard of them. There's "Biffo, the Sad Clown" and "Aaaahhchu, the Choo Choo." I sort of like that one myself — oh, no, I didn't read it. Hey, I'm too old for that stuff, no matter what my mom thinks. What I liked about Mr. Davidson's book is the title. You know. A train called Aaaahhchu. Great name for a choo choo. Anyway, like I said, I'm too old for that stuff. I tell my mom that all the time, but she says I'm not. *(Shakes his head.)* You know mothers. I'll be her baby till I'm as old as Miss Biddle.

Now you take what Mrs. Davidson writes. *(Little smile, then:)* **Love. Passion. Romance.** *(Quickly)* **Says so right on the covers. Neat covers, too. Mr. Anderson has a few of her books down at the general store. He reads them. Yep. But he won't let me see them. I do get a peek now and then at the covers when Mr. A puts one of Mrs. D's books down to wait on a customer. I wonder if our library has any copies. I'll have to check.**

After I deliver to the Davidsons, it's on to Mr. Stoner's. You remember Mr. Stoner, our local architect. He's a really interesting guy. You should see his drawings and paintings. Besides being an architect, he's an artist. A lot of paintings and drawings of buildings and ... er ... women. Mr. Stoner is single, but he's dating Jenny Crabtree. I guess that's why most of the women in Mr. Stoner's pictures look like Miss Crabtree. She's the town librarian. Now you'd think with a name like Crabtree she'd be real ugly. No. She's not. She's really pretty. Makes a guy want to go to the library and take out a book or two — any book or two — preferably one by Mrs. Davidson. Yeah. Mr. Stoner is a lucky guy. They're getting married this coming June. She'll make a good looking June bride.

The whole town will come out for that wedding. That's how we are here. Give us a good wedding or a sad funeral and we'll come out in droves for it. After all, isn't that what life is all about anyway? Love and death, weddings and funerals. Passion and romance. People being born and people dying. *(He shrugs.)* **What do I know? My mom tells me I'm too big for my britches. But I tell her, "Mom, I'm not a kid anymore." I don't just deliver the newspaper. I read it. And even write in it once in a while. Mr. Ross, the publisher, says I have potential. He says *I* know something about real life. I do. At least, I think I do. I'm not just some little kid who delivers the**

paper. I'm growing up. Mom says I'm still a kid. *(Shrugs)* I'm not sure at times what I am. Maybe that's growing up for you. What do I know? *(Holds up a paper.)* All I know is what I read in the newspaper, and what I've learned delivering them. Hey, maybe someday I'll be a writer for our town's paper. We'll see. *(Checks his watch.)*

And speaking of newspapers, I have to deliver these before nine o'clock. *(Hops on his bicycle.)* The news must get through. See ya! *(Begins to ride around sign and flagpole.)* Extra! Extra! Read all about it! Site of future town war memorial chosen! *(Curtain as DANNY rides off.)*

The Trouble with Guys

PRODUCTION NOTES

PLAYER: 1 female.

PLAYING TIME: About 8 minutes.

COSTUME: Jeans, pretty blouse.

PROPERTIES: Phone, lipstick, eye shadow, make-up, tissues, comb, mousse.

SOUND EFFECTS: Romantic love song.

The Trouble with Guys

CHARACTER: KATIE, a teen-ager.

TIME: Saturday night.

SETTING: KATIE's room. KATIE sits behind her vanity looking through a frame where her mirror would be. A phone and radio are on vanity. Behind her are school pennants, posters of rock stars.

AT RISE: KATIE is making faces at herself in "mirror."

KATIE: Look at me. Why me? Why this face? Why couldn't I look like Melanie or Daryl or Madonna? Why couldn't I be born with a face like that? I don't know why I look like this. The cheekbones are all wrong. The hair is all wrong. The nose is . . . almost all wrong. The eyes are too big — or too small? *(Looking around)* **Maybe it's the lighting in here. They say it's all in the lighting.** *(Looking at her face in "mirror")*

Is it any wonder why all those movie stars look so beautiful, while girls like me have to look so . . . so . . . ordinary? I hate looking ordinary. Maybe I should have the eyes, the nose, and the cheekbones done. A little plastic surgery and I, too, could be a star, could look beautiful, instead of ordinary. I'll save up my McBurger paychecks and maybe in ten years — maybe — I'll have enough to have the lips puckered. That is if I don't need a new pair of shoes first. And knowing me, I probably will. *(Begins to apply her make-up, stops, then says the following before actually doing it.)*

It's up to you, Katie, to do a whole make over. It's your life. You don't deserve to be plain, ordinary. So here we go. A little dab here and a little dab there, a brush stroke here, a brush stroke there, some lipstick, some eye shadow, mousse, etc., etc., etc. In a few minutes, perhaps

hours, the old Katie will be buried under tons of chemicals, dyes, grease, lotion, and powder. And like Botticelli's Venus born out of the master's palette, I shall emerge out of this sea of glop into a living goddess. Or a reasonable facsimile thereof. *(Stops for a second.)*

I hate this. But it's either this or obscure anonymity, total rejection, and no date for Saturday night, which is tonight. *(Starts doing her make-up faster.)* And I do hate to sit home on Saturday nights. Actually I hate to sit home on any night, but especially Saturday night. *(As she applies make-up)* I am a person who likes to dance. *(Gets up and turns on her radio and dances around to romantic music as if with some guy.)* Dancing in the semidarkness with him. *(Looks at rock star posters and points to one.)* Or better yet, *him.* Yes! Me and *(Rock star's name)* alone at Danny's Dance-o-rama. The lights are low, the music's loud, we are hot. *(Rock star's name)* is totally and deeply in love with me — or a reasonable facsimile thereof. He doesn't care if I'm wearing make-up or if I've had extensive facial surgery. To *(Rock star's name)*, my cheekbones are perfect. He says, "Katie, what big eyes you have." And I say, "The better to see you with, my dear." And he says, "Katie, what a nice nose you have." And I say, "The better to smell you with, my dear." He's wearing Brute™. And last, but not least, as this really romantic song plays, reaching a crescendo, *(Rock star's name)* holds me tighter, looks down at me and says in this really romantic voice, *(She tries to sound romantically deep)* "Katie, what pretty lips you have." And guess what I say? *(Music stops and she sits back down.)* But then that's all just a fantasy. A dream.

In reality, in my life, real life, I'm stuck with Buck Brewster, high school football captain and chief bonehead. Why does he have to look so *cute* in his football uniform and act so *dumb* on a date? Can't he be smart and cute? Or is that against the rules? Guys! Why do I do this to my face to impress them? Because I don't want to sit home on a Saturday night? Because I don't want to be lonely? Because I don't want to end up an old maid like old Miss Diddlebocker who always chaperones our school dances?

Why do I do it? For love. Yeah. That's it. I do it all for L-O-V-E — love. Which spells evol — evil — backwards. Yes, love is evil. At least when you want to be beautiful and all you have to look forward to are zits and excessive fat in all the wrong places at all the wrong times. Like anytime I'm alive. *(Looks at her face.)* It's beginning to take on a whole new look. A new image. Is this me or what? This is going to be a face that launched a thousand ships, or at least a couple of jet skis. *(Shakes her head.)* I'm doing it all for you, boys.

Why can't a guy be more like a woman?! How does that line from *My Fair Lady* go ... er ... ? *(Thinks)* "Why can't a woman be like a man?" Sure. Great. Just what the world needs. More jocks. More auto mechanics. More football captains. Guys. They talk a great line. All so macho. And the way they walk. *(She gets up.)* How do they do it? Sort of like this. *(Imitates a real macho man.)* Emphasis on the swagger, a little swing of the hips, hands jivin', head wobbling. A little moon walk when switching into reverse. Cool. I'm cool. I'm a man. Watch out. I'm dangerous. *(She sits.)* It's a wonder they don't get cramps, twist an ankle, pop a knee.

And they hate dancing. Oh, they do it. But they hate it. "Football players don't dance," he tells me every Saturday night. "Wanna see a movie?" I always say yeah. And sure enough, we end up seeing either "Return of the Hacksaw Murderer" or "Blood on Delacey Street, VI or VII." Whatever happened to a nice love story? A little romance? Why do guys always want to take me to horror films? Are they trying to tell me something? Or do they just want me to jump in their lap. Oh, I know all you guys. You think we're all a bunch of wimps. Take us to a horror flick and we go to pieces. *(Feigns fear, pleading)* Oh, big guy, help me, I'm so scared. Excuse me, but can I jump into your lap? *(Serious)*

We all know what you boys are up to. But then again the last horror movie we went to, he just wanted to feed me popcorn and watch the film. I tried to tell him about my life, you know? The possible plastic surgery, the new nose, my job slinging burgers. All he wanted to do was count the bodies and eat popcorn. I mean is it *me?* Am I that uninteresting? That boring? I ask you, mirror, am I a woman or a wimp? And why can't I just stop all this whining and just get it over with? Go to the horror film, jump in his lap, make him happy. Why not? Isn't that what life is all about? Or do I want to become Ophelia and go to a nunnery? Nah.

I want to be loved, accepted. Doesn't everyone? I'm a normal young woman. Ergo, I am supposed to enjoy popcorn, horror films, and guys who crush soda cans in their bare hands. It's what every young girl dreams of: a guy who'll take you to a horror film and crush soda cans in his bare hands for your enjoyment. *(In deep voice)* This one's for you, babe. *(In her voice)* I hate it when they do that. And why must they all call us babe? My name is Katie. I like my name. I'm not some baby. Oh, look, I don't mean to be a grouch. Yes, I know, the guys think they're being so sweet when they say, *(In deep voice)* "So, babe, how's it goin'?" *(In her voice)* Don't laugh! He said that to me when he picked me up last Saturday night. *(Thinks, then)* You think maybe he was nervous? Couldn't think of what to say? He never talks much. Could he be scared of me? But he's captain of the football team. Do guys get nervous around girls? Maybe they do. Maybe that's why they try to be so macho, to cover up their fear. Gee. Maybe that's why they do a lot of things that seem so macho. They're all a bunch of wimps? Nah. They aren't wimps. They're just a little nervous, butterflies in the stomach and all. Maybe that's why he threw up after that last horror film we saw. Here I'm thinking it was all that blood and popcorn, and in reality he was afraid he'd look scared in front of me. *(Smiles)* Ahh. Could it be possible? Maybe that's why he started growing that mustache. *(Pauses and looks at herself.)*

Yeah. And look at me. Hair perfect, eyes perfect, lips pouting just right. I'm a killer! But why do I do it? Is it because I'm afraid of being left out? Looking unfeminine if I'm not covered with make-up? This is crazy! I'm a woman! I don't need all this stuff to look like one. And he doesn't have to crush soda cans in his bare hands to impress me. *(Begins to remove make-up.)* If he doesn't like me the way I am, he can just go to that dance alone tonight. I'll go to a play or a movie with Jerry. He keeps telling me about these plays and films he likes. He wanted me to see *Casablanca* with him down at the Little Theater. I think I'll call Jerry. I'm tired of horror films and football games. And Jerry is smart too. He's real smart. He's the editor of the school paper. *(Takes off final bit of make-up.)*

There. All off. Now let me just give Jerry a call. I'm in the mood for a little romance, and right now *Casablanca* sure sounds better than "Hacksaw Massacre on Bleaker Street." Actually *Casablanca* always sounds better than "Hacksaw Massacre on Bleaker Street." *(Curtain begins to fall as KATIE picks up phone and dials, listens, then)* Hi, Jerry. Yeah. It's me, Katie. I'm fine. How are you? Great. Do I want to see *Casablanca?* Well . . . let me see . . . *(Thinks a second, big smile.)* OK. Sure. *(Curtain)*

The Day Billy Died

PRODUCTION NOTES

PLAYERS: 5 males; 2 females.

PLAYING TIME: About 15 minutes.

COSTUMES: SAM in casual clothes. BILLY, RANDY, MANDY, and JAY in jeans, leather jackets, bright shirts, boots. LORI in jeans and casual clothes. In last scene, all but NARRATOR wear black. NARRATOR in jeans, leather jacket, motorcycle boots.

PROPERTIES: Chairs.

SETTING: NARRATOR sets each scene.

LIGHTING EFFECTS: Moonlight, spotlight, lights can come up and fade as mentioned in script.

SOUND EFFECTS: Drum roll, guitar chord, distant sounds of city, Billy's song.

The Day Billy Died

CHARACTERS: NARRATOR; BILLY; SAM, brother; RANDY, Billy's band member; MANDY, Billy's band member; JAY, Billy's band member; LORI, Billy's girlfriend.

TIME: Morning of the day BILLY died.
SETTING: Dark stage, spotlight comes up on chairs.
AT RISE: NARRATOR enters.

NARRATOR: *(Sadly)* **This is where Billy lives. It is the morning of the day Billy died. We are in the living room. His mom's coffee table is here.** *(Indicates Center Stage.)* **It has the family album on it, these chairs are really the sofa.** *(BILLY and SAM enter.)* **There's Billy now. And that's his brother, Sam. They were like most brothers: fought a lot as kids, but, at heart, they loved each other.** *(NARRATOR stands in shadows and watches.)*

SAM: **Bill, look at this.** *(Mimes picking up photo album.)* **The family photo album.**

BILLY: **I guess Mom had it out again, Sam. She's always showing Lori.**

SAM: **You going to marry that girl, or what?**

BILLY: **Someday, sure.**

SAM: **Like when?**

BILLY: **As soon as the band makes it.**

SAM: **You and your band. Are you going to marry Lori or not? You know she loves you.**

BILLY: **I know. And, yes, I'm going to marry her. If she'll have me. And if my band makes it.**

SAM: *(Mimes looking through album.)* **It will. Hey, look at this. Here we are with our first guitars. What were we? Five? Six?**

BILLY: **I was five, you were six.**

SAM: **I played around with that old Fender bass for a year, but you never put yours down.**

BILLY: Yeah. I couldn't get enough of it. *(They mime turning the page.)* Look at this. Here's Randy and me. Our first jam session. We must have been about seven or eight.

SAM: You guys were pretty good, too.

BILLY: We were kids.

SAM: But good. *(Mimes turning page.)* Look. Our little league team.

BILLY: Remember how I got on that team?

SAM: Yeah, I remember.

BILLY: You were this great pitcher. Mr. Johnson couldn't live without you on his team.

SAM: Old Mr. Johnson. What a guy. Look at him. Cap, uniform. He was really into baseball. He was a great guy.

BILLY: But a tough coach. And you were his number one pitcher. When I tried to get on his team, he said I was too short even for shortstop. But you stuck up for me. You told him unless I played on the team, you'd quit. The next thing I knew, I was between first and second base.

SAM: Second and third base.

BILLY: I was never really good at baseball.

SAM: The worst shortstop we ever had.

BILLY: I guess I was better with a guitar than with a baseball glove.

SAM: You're right. You sure were.

BILLY: *(Mimes turning page.)* Look at this.

SAM: Our boy scout troop. That was great. I used to love going on those camping trips.

BILLY: Singing around the campfire. That was the best.

SAM: Here you are with your guitar, singing old camp songs, no doubt.

SAM and BILLY: *(Singing together)* Down in the valley, the valley so low — *(Or)* [— Row, row, row your boat gently down the stream, merrily, merrily, merrily, life is but a dream.] Not exactly your top ten, but . . .

BILLY: I used to love those songs.

SAM: Me too. The good old days. *(Mimes turning page.)* **Look at this. Do you believe we once looked like this? I can't believe it.**

BILLY: **Fashions do change.**

SAM: **Thank goodness.**

BILLY: **You got that right.**

SAM: *(Mimes turning page, trying not to laugh.)* **Who's this, Billy boy?**

BILLY: **You jerk. Who put that in there?**

SAM: **Mom, no doubt.**

BILLY: **But you took it. Mr. Private Eye with your new camera.**

SAM: **Hey, it had a two hundred millimeter telephoto lens. I had to do something with it and that new electronic flash.**

BILLY: **Sure, sure. So, tell me, big brother — pun intended — how did you get that shot? What did you do? Follow me and Lori all night?**

SAM: **No, Billy. I just bumped into you and Lori that night.** *(He tries not to laugh.)*

BILLY: *(Punching him in the arm gently)* **Yeah, sure.**

SAM: **No, really.**

BILLY: **Sure.**

SAM: **Would I lie to you?**

BILLY: **All the time.**

SAM: **Well here's the truth: me and Jennifer just happened to be parked up on Lover's Peak and who drives up but my little baby brother and his cute girlfriend, the ever-present, since the second grade, Lori.**

BILLY: **And so you sneak up on us, wait for the big moment and nearly blind us with your electronic flash.**

SAM: **You had your eyes closed anyway. And look at this close-up. Look at that composition, those colors — those lips. What a lover. You kissed her nose.** *(He laughs.)*

BILLY: **Hey, it was dark. I had my eyes closed. I missed her lips.**

SAM: I bet you don't miss them anymore.

BILLY: *(Stands up.)* As a matter of fact, I miss them right now.

SAM: *(Mimes closing album and stands.)* You going to see her again tonight?

BILLY: Yep. Right after band practice. I can't wait to see her.

SAM: *(As BILLY and SAM exit.)* I'll bet.

NARRATOR: Little did Billy know it would be his last date with Lori. They had all these hopes and dreams for the future, but . . . *(NARRATOR can't speak for a moment as he hangs his head.)* So that's how Billy's last day began. That afternoon he met with the members of his band, Randy, Jay and Mandy. Our scene now changes. It is afternoon. There are drums here, a microphone here. We are at the place where Billy and his band rehearse. Here they come now. *(They enter as NARRATOR speaks.)* Randy has his guitar, Jay his sax, and Mandy has her drumsticks. *(RANDY, JAY and MANDY walk about. RANDY mimes carrying guitar, JAY mimes carrying a sax. MANDY sits behind "drums" and mimes doing a drum roll which we hear.)* Billy is a bit late. But he'll be here shortly with his guitar.

MANDY: So where's Billy boy?

RANDY: Probably with Lori again.

JAY: Are those two Siamese twins, or what?

RANDY: Yeah, right. Those two are never apart.

JAY: Inseparable.

MANDY: It's so romantic.

JAY and RANDY: Women.

MANDY: I think it's great he and Lori are so in love. The world needs more of that.

JAY: What we need, Mandy, is a hit record, but first, more practice. And without our lead singer, we can't — *(Just then BILLY enters, he mimes carrying his guitar.)* Here he is now.

BILLY: Sorry, guys. I got caught in traffic. Some drunk

wracked up his car and —

MANDY: Was anyone hurt?

BILLY: Just the drunk. Nothing fatal.

RANDY: This time.

JAY: Look, guys. If we're ever going to get on MTV, we'd better start practicing.

BILLY: Right.

MANDY: Hey, Billy, did that guy from the record company ever call you back?

BILLY: Yeah. Didn't I tell you?

RANDY, JAY, MANDY: No! What did he say?!

BILLY: Yes!

RANDY, JAY, MANDY: All right!

RANDY: When do we cut the demo?

BILLY: Would you believe he said whenever it's convenient for us?

MANDY: You're kidding? He said that?

BILLY: Believe it. He loves us.

RANDY, JAY, MANDY: All right!

BILLY: I told you we were going to make it. You just have to hang in there. Never give up.

MANDY: That's what you keep telling us.

RANDY: He's been right so far.

JAY: Frankly, I'm amazed. I never thought we'd even get that first professional gig.

MANDY: I know. Imagine, people actually wanting to pay us money to do this.

BILLY: Don't tell anyone, but I'd do it for nothing.

RANDY: I know what you mean. I just want to play.

MANDY: I have to. I can't help it.

JAY: I know. Music is in my blood.

BILLY: You've got that right. So what are we going to record on that demo? Our agent wants to send it to all the record companies. We have to make it count.

RANDY: How about that one you wrote about Detroit, Billy?

JAY: No. We should do the new rap song he wrote. Isn't that our biggest request at all the dances? Right, Bill?

BILLY: Look, even though I wrote it, I think we should do that other one: the one we all worked on together.

MANDY: If you ask me, I think we should record that new love song you wrote for Lori. It's beautiful. I wish someone would write something like that for me, you know, guys, you know? Huh?

JAY: Forget it.

RANDY: Yeah, don't hold your breath, Mandy.

MANDY: Thanks a lot.

BILLY: They're only kidding, Mand.

JAY: We are? *(MANDY glares at them.)*

RANDY: We are.

JAY: We're kidders at heart.

RANDY: *(Getting too close to MANDY)* Mandy, did I ever tell you female drummers turn me on?

MANDY: *(Pushes him away.)* Yeah. Too bad bass guitar players like you don't turn me on, Randolph.

RANDY: *(Mimes doing a bass chord with his guitar, which we hear.)* I told you never to call me that!

BILLY: Guys, guys, come on. We have to practice. If you want, we'll do the love song. But for now, we have to practice. We have the prom, that gig at Max's, and if we don't get these tunes down, we aren't going to be on MTV.

MANDY: I can't wait. Look out Madonna, here I come.

JAY: Here *we* come, Mandy.

RANDY: Yeah, we're a band. Not a solo act.

MANDY: I was only dreaming.

BILLY: Hey, we all have to dream. We're going to be on MTV, Lori and I are going to get married. I'm going to ask her.

JAY: Yeah, but when?

BILLY: Maybe tonight when I see her after practice.

RANDY: Keep dreaming. You won't ask her. You'll chicken out.

MANDY: No he won't. That's Billy's dream. Don't ruin it for him. You've got to have a dream. Right, Billy?

BILLY: Right. And I say again — no MTV if we don't practice. So let's do it. *(Lights die out as we hear band play part of Billy's love song then exit as next scene is set up and NARRATOR talks.)*

NARRATOR: They never got on MTV. Not Billy. Not his band. And they had so many dreams. Did he ever marry Lori? Let's just say that all dreams don't come true no matter how hard you want them too. Even I wish things could have been different that day, but they weren't. *(Lights come up.)* It's now evening. This is the park where Billy is going to meet Lori. Moonlight mystifies the night. The distant sounds of the city can be heard drifting in over the trees. And *(Points to chairs, which he arranges like a bench)* this is a park bench. This is the park bench where Billy and Lori spent their last moments together. I'll never forget it. It will always be burned into my brain. Here they come now. *(NARRATOR stands in shadow as BILLY and LORI enter arm in arm.)*

LORI: So how was practice?

BILLY: OK.

LORI: Just OK?

BILLY: Pretty good.

LORI: Pretty good. Billy, you have to be the humblest guy I ever met. Most other guys in a band like yours would be bragging all over school how great they were, but not you.

BILLY: *(Shrugs)* Hey, I'm a humble guy. What do you want from me?

LORI: I know. *(Kisses him.)* That's why I love you. So what are you going to play at the prom? *(They sit down, close.)*

BILLY: A few of our new tunes. And some of the old ones.

LORI: Great. You really write some beautiful songs.

BILLY: I wrote a new one.

LORI: Great. What's it about?

BILLY: You.

LORI: Me? You wrote a song for me?

BILLY: Yeah, why not?

LORI: *(She looks down for a moment.)* **You never say much about how you feel about me.**

BILLY: **I guess I'm a writer and not a talker. So I wrote you this song.**

LORI: **How's it go?**

BILLY: **You want to see it?**

LORI: **Sure. Of course I do.**

BILLY: *(Afraid to hand her some sheet music, which he mimes taking out of back pocket and holding.)* **I hope you like it.**

LORI: *(Waiting to be given it)* **Are you going to give that sheet music to me or what?**

BILLY: *(Mimes handing it to her.)* **Oh, right. Here.**

LORI: *(Mimes reading it, then)* **You wrote this for me?**

BILLY: **You like it?**

LORI: **Like it?** *(Hugs him tight, then)* **I love it. And I love you.** *(They kiss, then)* **No one has ever been so nice to me before. I can't believe you wrote this for me.**

BILLY: **Well, believe it. And guess what?**

LORI: **You're going to be on MTV.**

BILLY: **No.**

LORI: **Oh, yes, you will. You will. I just know you will.** *(NARRATOR looks down sadly, knowing the truth.)*

BILLY: **Maybe. But we're going to be recording that demo.**

LORI: **Terrific. What song are you going to use?**

BILLY: **The guys want me to use** *(Points to the "sheet music")* **this one.**

LORI: **I don't know what to say. I can't believe this is all happening.**

BILLY: **Hey, sometimes good things happen, you know. We worked hard enough for it.**

LORI: **I know. You're always practicing. Sometimes we can't be together because of it.**

BILLY: **Don't worry, that's all going to change.** *(BILLY puts his arm around LORI and they sit closer without speaking for a* *few moments, then)* **Lori.**

LORI: Yeah?

BILLY: There's something I want to ask you.

LORI: About what?

BILLY: About us.

LORI: Yeah? What?

BILLY: We've been together for a long time now. Right?

LORI: Let's see ... I met you in the second grade. I believe you were the cute little boy who used to tie my braids together. Was that you, Billy?

BILLY: *(Trying not to laugh)* Yeah, that was me. I must confess, I did get a charge out of tying your braids together.

LORI: I know you did. So it's agreed. We've been friends for ages.

BILLY: Right. Agreed.

LORI: So then what do you want to ask me? If I love you? Well, the answer to that is yes.

BILLY: I know. That's not it.

LORI: Billy, will you tell me? The suspense is killing me. What do you want to ask me?

BILLY: *(Mimes taking out a ring box.)* Look, I know we haven't graduated yet, but we will soon, and I will be going to college to study composing, but I want us to always be together. So I was sort of wondering ...

LORI: Yes ... yes ...

BILLY: You think you'd want to marry me like when we graduate or something?

LORI: *(Hugs him.)* I think so. Yes.

BILLY: Great. *(Mimes handing her the "ring box.")* This is for you.

LORI: *(Mimes opening box and looks at ring, takes it out.)* Oh, Billy, a ring, it's beautiful.

BILLY: You like it? It's not very big.

LORI: It's big enough. *(They hug and kiss as lights dim out on them and come up on NARRATOR.)*

NARRATOR: It was a beautiful moment, that night in the park. I was there, too. A bunch of us guys were hanging out. You know how it is. A warm spring Saturday night, school almost over, nothing to do. So you fool around, have a little fun. Anyway, Billy walked Lori to the bus stop before he headed out to a gig he had at a local club with his band. But he never got there. *(Pause)* Our scene changes again, from the park to the cemetery. It's only a few days later. *(Points to chairs as he rearranges them.)* These are tombstones. Flowers are everywhere, especially here. Someone has just been buried. Billy. His friends and brother are coming. *(RANDY, JAY, MANDY, SAM and LORI enter and stand around, holding each others' hands.)* I guess I told you that Billy never made it to MTV, he never married Lori, and the band eventually broke up. *(LORI mimes laying flowers on Billy's "grave.")* Lori was shattered, heartbroken, as was everyone who knew Billy. Anyway, after a long depression, Lori found another guy and got married. She has two kids now. But she still thinks of Billy. So do I. I can never forget him. Or that last day — the day Billy died. I keep seeing it over and over again. It's like this little play that keeps going on over and over and over again in my mind. I'm always the Narrator. And the play never ends. It just keeps playing over and over again, day in and day out in my mind. Why? *(He looks down, then at audience.)* Well, you remember that last night in the park when Billy proposed to Lori? I told you I was there too? A bunch of us guys were. We were hanging out, drinking. I only had one or two. I swear. I wasn't drunk. I swear. Anyway, after we finished the six pack, which I didn't even buy, I hopped onto my motorcycle and drove off. Hey, I was fine. I tell you I was not drunk. I tell everyone that. Everyone. *(Pause)* Look, I paid my debt to society for what happened. I was hurt, too, in the accident. But they say I killed Billy. He never knew what hit him. I just came racing out of the park and there he was. Right in front of me. I couldn't think fast enough to avoid him. I hit him, but I wasn't drunk! It was just an accident! But I keep seeing this play over and over again in my head. *(He watches as a tearful LORI on her knees, mimes fixing flowers on BILLY's grave.)* I'm really sorry about all this. You know? I wish I could change it, make it have a happy ending, but I can't. No matter what I do, this is the ending I'm stuck with. I'm really sorry. Honest, I am. *(Pause, softly)* Real sorry. *(Lights dim out as some of BILLY's love song fades out and NARRATOR stares at the grave.)*

Why I Want to Be an Actor

PRODUCTION NOTES

PLAYER: 1 male or female.

PLAYING TIME: 12 minutes with the music.

COSTUME: Leotards or something flashy for audition.

LIGHTING EFFECTS: Spotlight follows JAMIE.

SOUND EFFECTS: 3 music cassettes for song backup, dance music, and gymnastic routine.

Why I Want to Be an Actor

CHARACTER: JAMIE.

TIME: Today.

SETTING: Empty stage in a theater.

AT RISE: JAMIE enters and stands Center Stage in spotlight. JAMIE looks at audience as if it were the person JAMIE is auditioning for. A spotlight is on JAMIE.

JAMIE: Hi. My name is Jamie. And I want to be an actor. *(Pause)* Why do I want to act? I have to. It's in my blood, you know. I have to be out there in front of people. I have to perform. Even when I was a small child, I'd dance for my parents and grandparents. I loved to sing. They would applaud. But I didn't do it for the applause. I just did it because I like to. I've always been an extrovert. I'm not the life-of-the-party type, but I do like to make people laugh — and think — which is why I like acting. And they applauded. *(Thinks, then)*

Even as a little kid, I knew all the songs on the radio and all the dances on TV. I could sing all the Broadway show tunes. I saw *A Chorus Line* four or five times. And *The Fantastics* maybe three times. What can I say? They're Broadway. *(Pause)*

I love the movies too: drama, comedies, musicals. And plays. *(Pause)* I live to see the plays on Broadway, off-Broadway, off-off-Broadway. As long as it's in the general vicinity of Broadway, I have to see it.

It's always amazing to me the way those actors and actresses remember all those lines, all those words. How do they do it? And who thought up all of those words? Where do they get them from? Then I realized where it all came from. *(Covers heart.)* Right here. From inside. From real life and how it hit them. And now they will always be remembered for their words or their performances. That's great, you know. To be remembered.

I love going to museums. I was in the Metropolitan Museum of Art the other day. All that history. Thousands of years of sculpture, painting. Praxiteles, Renoir, Da Vinci. They left their mark.

We're all here for such a short time. Most people lead lives of quiet desperation, you know, as Thoreau said. I don't want to leave just a pile of dust behind when I go. I want to leave a piece of me behind that others can look at and say, that was a person who cared. Yeah, I want to leave my mark. And not just my named carved in some park bench in some park. Maybe this all sounds a little egotistical, but I just want to create something, something worth something. Something with meaning. I don't want to just pass through life like a sleepwalker. *(Pauses, then)*

Most people I know are interested in adventure films or horror movies. Me? I want to go to the theater or to the ballet. Even the opera. At first, I didn't know what they all meant. Like opera. The operas are always in French, German or Italian. But then I began to read the librettos, the words in English, as I listened to the music. Talk about drama. Rigoletto, Carmen, Aida, La Boheme — these are about real life, love, death, heartbreak. I couldn't believe it. People laugh at opera, but they don't know what they are really about. Mainly love, unrequited love. Suddenly opera took on a whole new meaning.

I started taking voice lessons, dance lessons and acting lessons. That's what I spend my money on. I want to perform. *(As if listening to person JAMIE's auditioning for)* Can I sing? Well, yes. Do you want to hear? You do? OK. Yes, I gave the tape to your assistant. Ready? Then let's

do it. *(To someone Offstage)* **Music please.** *(Tape of music to a popular song is played as JAMIE sings beautifully.)* **That's it. Yeah, I love to sing. I do it all the time — on my way to school, in the hallways, at home in the shower, in school musicals.** *(Listens, then)*

Can I dance? I take classes in ballet, jazz and modern dance. You still want to know if I can dance? Yes, I gave your assistant my dance music tape, too. Are you ready? OK. *(To Offstage)* **Dance music please.** *(JAMIE dances to another popular song.)* **That's it. I love to dance as much as I love to sing.** *(Walks around as spotlight follows JAMIE.)*

I have a lot of energy, I guess. I never want to stop. Yeah, I'm very athletic. I'm on the school's gymnastics team. You want to see my routine? No? Just a few cartwheels, tumbles, etc? OK. Yeah, I brought that tape too. You want to see just a few moments of the routine, not the whole thing. No problem. OK. *(To someone Offstage)* **Exercise music. That's tape three.** *(Modern or classical music plays as JAMIE does routine.)* **That's it.**

Am I nervous? Yeah. Alway a little nervous on stage, but that's what gives me the energy to act, you know. It drives me. I once wanted to be a stand-up comic. Don't laugh. It's true. I used to tell all these jokes, only they weren't jokes, they were just funny stories. My friends used to laugh at the things that would come out of my mouth. I have no idea where they came from, but people were laughing. So, I figured I'd try stand up. Yeah, I gave it my best shot, but it wasn't really what I wanted to do for the rest of my life.

What I really want to do is make people think and feel something. Acting is what I really want to do. Acting gives you the chance to be all these great people. You get to bring a part of yourself into the roles, that is if you're any good. If you just memorize the lines, the words, you're not an actor. You have to feel the words, know who you

are and who your character is. You have to become one with them. You must lose yourself in them. Well, not entirely lose yourself. There has to be more of a blending of you and the character you are playing. At first you wonder if it's possible, you know. You also begin to wonder who you are. You have to look at yourself, but not in the mirror. That only shows the outside you. You need to know the inner you. Who you really are.

So who am I? A person with a dream. As I said, I want to leave something more than just a pile of dust behind. So, I have this dream. A dream to be an actor. It's a wonderful dream, but then the reality begins to creep in: does anyone else want me to be an actor? I ask myself: What about Mom and Dad? What about my teachers? What about the directors and the producers? The critics? And what about the public — the audience? Do they care? Do they want me? That is the real question. All I know is I just want a chance to show my parents, the directors, the producers, the critics and the audience what I can do. And I know I can do it. I can act. Actually, I have to act. It's in my blood. I know it sounds corny, but that's how I feel. *(Pause)* I want to be part of all this. I want to fit in. I'm always worried that I won't fit in, or be picked for a part. Am I too short, too tall, too old, too young, too fat, too thin? Am I the right color? *(Shakes head.)*

That's what I hate. Being right for the part. I'm an actor. I can make the part mine. My age, my weight, my height, my color should not matter. But it does. I know I can't play a baby. I'm too old for that — or am I? I took this acting class once, you know. I played a tree *(Waving arms like big branches)* waving my branches in the wind, and I was *(Twirls and falls slowly to ground)* a leaf falling, falling in spirals to the ground. *(Stands and tap dances across stage.)* I played rain, pitter patting on the ocean. *(Moves whole body in waves.)* I even played the ocean moving in waves. I was so good, everyone threw up! *(Points to self.)* I made them all seasick! Do I have a sense of humor? You have to have a sense of humor to play a raindrop. So I can also play a baby. *(Curls up on floor, then kicks and cries, then gets up.)* I can do it all. No, I don't need to be burped. I was that good, you thought I might! *(Laughs)* No. *(Holds stomach.)* I'm ... er ... fine.

So, I just want to fit in. I want to be wanted by millions. Do I want to make a lot of money? Of course I want to make a lot of money, but I'd do it for nothing. Yes, I know you don't pay much. Listen, I once played a grape in a school play for twenty performances and I did it for nothing. I became a grape. I ate grapes, drank grape juice, watched Fruit of the Loom commercials. I was going to be the best grape there ever was.

Hey, maybe one day I could become a star — a California raisin! You know what they say. There are no small parts, just small actors. And I'm not small. I have a dream and even if it means I have to become a grape, I'll be the best grape you ever saw. Dancing and singing in a bowl of fruit if you want. I'd prefer to be the top banana, but if the only role is a grape, I'm the only grape you'll want.

Do I work hard at school? Yeah. I try. I work after class, too. Yeah, right. Waiting tables. What else, right? All the money goes for acting and dance lessons. And books. I love reading plays. I once joined this book club that published nothing but new Broadway play scripts. I read all the big ones and a few small ones. The books were a lot cheaper than the tickets.

Do my parents help? Dad's a cop and my mother's a secretary. They do what they can. *(Pause)* Do I want to impress them? *(Thinks)* I just want to act. If that impresses them, I'll be happy. All I know is I gotta be me, as the song goes. I just have to act. I'll keep going out on these auditions until I get the chance. Until I get my big break.

Yes, I've been to a few auditions. Yes, open auditions like this one. I haven't been invited to any closed auditions yet — but I will. Wait, you'll see. Someday all the neon lights on Broadway will be spelling out *(Looking up as if at a big sign)* J-A-M-I-E — Jamie, in bright lights, some red, some blue, some green, and some bright white — but all flashing *Jamie, Jamie, Jamie.* That'll be me. Oh, I know I'm me now. But I want the world to know. All I know is I'll never give up till I make it. You have to trust in yourself, you know. You have to have a dream. You have to hang in there. Take all the rejections in stride and go right on to the next audition. So here I am. What do you think? Do I get the part? *(Listens, then)* You'll call me? Right. You want my number? You do? Great! It's 555-555-5217. Yeah, I know I came a long way, but here I am. On Broadway. Maybe. Thanks. You'll call me. Maybe. I'll be waiting. *(Exits)*

Bye, Bye, Baby

PRODUCTION NOTES

PLAYER: 1 female.

PLAYING TIME: About 8 minutes.

COSTUME: Casual clothes.

Bye, Bye, Baby

CHARACTER: KIM, a teen-aged single mother.

TIME: Today.
SETTING: An empty stage.
AT RISE: KIM enters and paces back and forth.

KIM: *(Pacing in thought, then looks at audience.)* **What choice did I have? What choice? Huh? Can you tell me? Can you? Can anyone? You think this was easy for me? Well, it wasn't.** *(Stops and looks at audience.)* **It was the hardest thing I ever had to do; the hardest thing I ever did. The hardest, you know. I'm just a kid. I know, I know. I try to keep that a secret. I try to act all grown up. But I'm just a kid. I do try really hard to act like I'm all grown up. And in ways I am. But part of me is still a little kid. So I make mistakes. I screw up once in a while.** *(Thinks, looks down, then)* **I'm just a kid.** *(Looks up at audience.)* **That's what everyone tells me. You have school, Kim. Your life. You have no time for a baby. You have to graduate. Yeah, I have to graduate, go to college. I want to. I do. I want to get a good job. Make something of myself. I want to. I have to. You have to be independent these days. You can't just wait around for someone else to take care of you. You can't expect to be taken care of. You have to do it yourself. You have to decide to take control of your life. And only I can make those choices for me, to do those things. That's what everyone says. They all say it: my parents, the counselors, the people at the agency, the people at the hospital.** *(To audience)* **You can't keep your baby, they all say. I can't. How could I? I'm just a kid.** *(Silent then)* **I don't know. I don't know. I don't feel like a kid.** *(Thinks, then)* **Did I do the right thing? I'll never see her again. Never.** *(Looks up at audience.)* **That's what hurts**

– 39 –

the most, you know. What if she misses me? I am her natural mother. I miss her. *(Thinks)* Maybe she'll look for me when she gets old enough. I don't know. I want to see her. Even now I want to see her, even if for just one last time. *(Pause)* I never wanted this to happen. But it did.

I was in love. We both were. We were so in love, you know. At least we thought we were. We had all these plans. *(Frowns)* Then he found out he wasn't ready to be a father. He wanted to see Disney World, play football, have some fun. He said he was sorry. Sorry. Sorry? That's what he told me. I'm sorry, Kim. Sorry. So he left. He said he wasn't responsible. It was my fault anyway. But he was there too. Or was he? Maybe I was just there. His head was somehere else. Maybe those dreams we had were just my dreams. I don't know. He said he loved me.

We were going to go through Lamaze together, you know. Breathe, breathe, breathe. The whole thing. But no. We didn't. I went by myself. Alone. Me and my pillow and my baby. *(Smiles, holds her stomach.)* She could kick. Really restless. Like her mom, you know. *(Silent)*

Before all this happened, I was just another kid at school. I was alway so full of energy. Just couldn't relax. Into everything. I joined the gymnastics team, the track team, the cheerleading squad, the band. I was always doing something. Trying to keep busy. Stay out of trouble. I had a lot of energy to burn. We'd practice our routines at school on the athletic field. *(Does the routine.)* One, two, three, four, rush 'em, rush 'em, rush 'em — score! *(Thinks, then)* Or: Team, team, team, team, hit 'em hard — hit 'em mean! We had a million cheers. We'd practice them over and over again, till we got them just right, which wasn't that hard. Well, not for me. But a few of the girls weren't as coordinated as I am. They'd trip, fall, mess up the words. Their feet would get all tangled up. Their hands would end up all out of sync with their feet and the words. They were sort of klutzy, they'd mess up. Not me. Well . . . not at practice anyway. Now when it comes to real life . . . At practice, we'd help each other until we had each cheer just right. That's how it was at school, you know. We'd help each other out.

But this is different. Real different. You do it all by yourself. Oh, sure, everyone tries to help with advice. Eat this, don't eat that, drink this, don't drink that. Be careful. Think of the baby. Think of the baby. What do they think I've been thinking of for the last nine months? And now? And forever? Do they think I will ever forget her? Ever? How could I? She was my baby. She is my baby. She's a part of me. She'll always be a part of me. A part of me. Me. You know? She'll always be a part of me, no matter where she is. She wasn't some little teddy bear, some toy, she was part of me. She still is. And will always be. *(Pause, then)*

They tell you it's going to be hard, but you'll get over it. You'll get over it, they say. That's what they say. I hope they're right. I sure hope so. Because it is hard. It's hard. It hurts, you know. I keep thinking, does she miss me? Does she want me to hold her? Does she want me to feed her? Is she cold? Does she want me to tell her a story? Nurse her? *(Thinks)* I wanted to nurse her. I did in the hospital. *(Smiles)* Yeah, I did. She was hungry. Real hungry. *(Silent)* I miss her. God, I miss her. It does hurt. At times, it hurts so much, it scares me. I know I did the right thing. She'll have a better life with her new family. A better life than I could give her. At least right now. Yeah, I know I did the right thing. But it still hurts. I feel like someone I loved just died. And I can't bring them back. *(Thinks, then)*

At least when a parent or a grandparent dies, you know they loved you, they knew you. They shared your life. You may have lost them, and it hurts, but you still have all those great memories, you know. Memories of a happy life together. I wanted that for me and my baby.

She'll never have any memories of me. Of us. *(Pause, then tries to laugh.)* **I could have shown her how to do tumbles, cartwheels, help her in school, teach her how to sing and dance.** *(Pause)* **My cheers. About guys. But not now.** *(Thinks, then)*

I wonder if her new parents will do all those things. I hear they are nice people. Real nice. She's not able to have kids. He's a lawyer. They have a nice house in the suburbs. They can give her a lot of things I can't give her. But I would have tried. I would have. I would have tried to get a good job so I could buy her things. I would have tried to give her a good life. I would have tried. *(Thinks)*

How did this happen? Life is full of surprises. You think you're going through life with no real problems. Everything is going pretty well — OK. Sure, once in a while, you're miserable. Once in a while. Your guy starts seeing someone else. You hate your new homeroom teacher or he or she hates you. You have a fight with your mom, your best friend. But in general everything is going OK. You can sing all the latest songs, do all the latest dances. The guys think you're all right. One or two really want you. They call you all the time. You are feeling pretty good. Special. You know? You think nothing can go wrong. But then one day, or night, it does. And the next thing you know, here you are being scrutinized by doctors, nurses, counselors. Lawyers want to talk with you; they want you to sign papers. Lots of papers. Everyone wants to give you advice. Everyone is talking to you, but guess who isn't? Right. Him. Suddenly the calls stop, you're avoided in school, he is seen with someone else. And you're on your own. *(Pause)*

When I was a kid, things weren't so complicated. Then it was me and my dolls. Now it's just me. I should have kept her. I should have. But I signed the papers. I did the right thing. The right thing for her. They say I did the right thing for me, too. But I'm not so sure I did. I feel so bad about this. I called the lawyer, but he said it was final. The papers were signed and the baby was with her new mom and dad. But I'm her mom, I told him. I told him I just wanted to know if she was all right. He assured me she was, but that he could not divulge any further information. It was all confidential. But I'm her mother, I said. I told him, you know. He just said it was final. Did I understand what that meant? Of course, I understand what final means, I told him. What does he think I am? An idiot? He repeated that I had signed all the papers and to please not call back anymore. It was final. Then he hung up. He hung up, on me, the mother.

I tried to call the agency, but they said the same thing. It was final. So I guess it is. Final. You don't really know what that word "final" means until it's your baby they are talking about. Then it hits you here. *(Holds her heart.)* Finally. Like a ton of bricks. *(Silent, then)* They assured me I'd get over this empty feeling. All the counselors did. But they said it's going to take time. Time. How much time? I asked. That's different for everyone, they said. Some take a little longer than others to get over it, but you will. They assured me I would get over it. I am young. You have school, dances, friends. You'll get over it. But I don't think I ever will. I'll always be wondering where she is, how she's doing. *(Stops to think, then)* What if she gets sick and dies? I'm sorry. I don't mean to be morbid. But if she dies, I'll never know. I'll never know my own daughter has died. I won't be there to help her. To hold her hand. To tell her it will be all right. *(Pause, then)* I hope she's all right. God, let her be all right. Please. Let her grow up healthy and let her be happy. Let her have a happy life. Please, God. *(Can't talk, then)*

I want her back! I want my baby back! I hate this!

It's not fair. It's not fair. I don't even know her name. I was going to name her, but they told me not to. Don't get too attached. What a laugh! I'm nursing her for three days in the hospital and they tell me not to get too attached. So what do I do now? Mom wants me to go shopping with her. But I don't feel like going shopping, which is unlike me, you know. I love to shop. I was going to buy her a little dress for a going away present. But they told me not to. It was better to just let go. Let her go. So I let her go. *(Thinks, then)*

That last day my mom was there with me. She was holding my hand and I was holding my baby's tiny hand. We both hugged her and then the nurse took her out of my arms and held her as if to let us get one last look. *(Pauses)* We were all in tears. *(Pauses)* I kissed my baby once more, for the last time, and the nurse walked out with her. She just turned and walked out. I could hear the nurse's footsteps disappear down the long hallway. I heard a door slam. I just mumbled something. Then said, "Bye, bye, baby." And me and my mom hugged each other and cried. *(Silently stands there all alone for a few moments, then she walks off saying the final sentence making it sound final.)* That's all I could say. Bye, bye, baby. *(Curtain)*

DUOLOGS

The Emergency Room

PRODUCTION NOTES

PLAYERS: 1 female; 1 male.

PLAYING TIME: 8 minutes.

COSTUMES: Both in white, with slightly bloodstained white lab coats.

SOUND EFFECTS: Occasional voices on hospital intercom paging doctors, sound of distant ambulance siren.

The Emergency Room

CHARACTERS: DR. JANET ROSEN, a young doctor; DR. RON HERNANDEZ, an older doctor and head of emergency room staff.

TIME: Midnight.

SETTING: The doctors' lounge in a big city hospital. Medical charts and books, magazines and chairs are at rear of stage. Distant sound of an ambulance siren, voice on intercom paging doctors.

AT RISE: JAN enters. She paces. She is very upset. She sits, then gets up and paces again.

JAN: *(Pacing)* **It's just too much. It's not worth it. I just can't take this much longer. I knew it would be rough working in the emergency room of a big city hospital, but this is too much. They just keep hurting each other, shooting, stabbing. Killing. What can I do? I can't help them all. Some are just too far gone. It's too much. This is not what I thought being a doctor was going to be like. All this senseless killing and death.** *(RON enters.)*

RON: **Jan! Are you all right?**

JAN: *(A bit sarcastic)* **Yes, Doc Hernandez. I'm just great. I'm fine. Wonderful.** *(Looks at RON.)* **I just lost a kid. A little kid!**

RON: **You did the best you could.**

JAN: **Well, it just wasn't good enough, was it? It just wasn't good enough. Not this time.**

RON: **It was the best you could do. It was the best any of us could have done.**

JAN: **Why do people do that to each other? All the shooting and stabbing.**

RON: **That's life in the big city. It happens every day.** *(Checks his watch.)* **And night.**

JAN: **That kid was only six or seven. She was caught in a crossfire. Do you believe it? A crossfire! What are we** living in here? A war zone?

RON: Yes. We are.

JAN: I hate it, you know? I just hate it. It's so senseless.

RON: I hear you.

JAN: We can't help them.

RON: We do what we can.

JAN: I went to medical school to learn how to help people, to save lives. I always wanted to be a doctor.

RON: Same here. From the time I was old enough to watch Medic on TV, I said that's what I want to do when I'm old enough. So here I am. Here we are.

JAN: I know. Being a doctor always meant so much to me. I was going to save lives, help the sick, save the dying. I never thought of the other part of it. I never thought of what it was going to be like telling two crying parents that their baby is dead. Never.

RON: It's rough.

JAN: Rough? You should have seen them. They were hysterical.

RON: I know. I could hear the mother screaming all the way down the hall. You never get used to that part of it. And when it's a little kid that doesn't make it, it's even harder.

JAN: She never had a chance. And if she did make it, she would have never been the same. I tried to get her heart going. We got the tubes in, the IV lines; we got her breathing. And we kept (*Punching her fist into her open palm*) pounding away, pounding away on her chest. But CPR didn't help. We zapped her a few times with the defibrillator. But no use. She was just not going to come back.

RON: I saw her. You did all you could. All any of us could.

JAN: All I could do wasn't good enough. Not good enough.

RON: Was she your first kid?

JAN: The first that died on me. She reminded me of my little niece. Did you see what she had with her?

RON: The doll?

JAN: Yes. It was locked in her little hand. I was going to take it away, but I stopped. I know she was unconscious, but I just couldn't take that doll away from her.

RON: That's OK.

JAN: It was filthy. But it was hers. I just couldn't take it away from her. I should have taken it away from her. That's proper procedure. But I couldn't.

RON: You did what you thought was best for her.

JAN: For her? Or for me?

RON: Jan, you're a good doctor. This city needs good doctors like you. You can't get too emotionally involved. If you do, you'll go crazy.

JAN: But she was only a baby! What do you want me to do? Pull out the tubes, turn off all the switches and just pronounce her dead? As if she were some inanimate object? Well, I can't. I just can't treat a little kid as if she were some object. I have feelings too, you know.

RON: We all have feelings. No one here is doing this for fun or profit. We do it because we want to help people. I do. You do. We all do. All the nurses and doctors. That is what we have decided to do with our lives. That is what we have been trained for. And we all get upset when we lose someone, especially a little kid.

JAN: She'll never grow up, never fall in love, never. She's just gone. In a week I'll probably forget her.

RON: No you won't.

JAN: I will. There are too many of them to remember.

RON: Jan. Why did you come here?

JAN: *(Looks at him.)* Why? To help those who need help. But I never thought we'd be trying to save children caught in machine gun crossfire. What is wrong with these people? Don't they feel anything? How could they shoot a child?

RON: It happens.

JAN: I guess it does. Drunks and drive-bys. Drugs and bullets.

Senseless. Last week we had a twelve-year-old in here that was hit by some drunk, out-of-his-mind driver. We saved that kid. But he'll never walk again. And with all the head trauma, the brain injury, he may not be able to do much else either. But we saved him. Wonderful. Isn't medical science wonderful?

RON: It's all we have, the best we have right now. We do what we can. It's us against all the bullets, all the drunk drivers, all the knives, all the drugs, and all the disease. We are all there is. We are all these people have. It's you and me and this hospital. You know, Jan? Us. We are all those people have. And you did the best you could for that child. I mean, didn't you? Think about it. You did all you could for her. Right?

JAN: Yes.

RON: You're darn right you did. You weren't thinking about your next shopping spree at Macy's or playing racquetball, were you?

JAN: No.

RON: Of course you weren't. All you were thinking of was saving that kid's life, pulling her through, putting her back together, returning her to her mom and dad happy and healthy.

JAN: Yes, I was. But I didn't.

RON: No, you didn't. And there are going to be a lot more you can't save. But you can't give up trying. You have to do what you can, give it your best shot.

JAN: But it all seems so hopeless. Like last night. They brought in this little old woman. She must have been nearly eighty. Frail, you know? Tiny. Probably on Social Security. Just getting by. Some slime mugs her. Beats her half to death. She was barely breathing when EMS brought her in. We tried to save her, but we couldn't. Three hours later the cops bring in her alleged assailant, as they call the creep. He was shot trying to escape. Shot three times. Him we saved. He will live happily ever after. You know what he got from her? Four dollars. And he gets to live.

RON: That's how it goes sometimes. You just have to do the best you can, no matter who it is you're working on.

JAN: I do try. Really, I do.

RON: I know you do.

JAN: But it's not easy.

RON: No one said it was going to be easy. Doctors have to make some tough decisions and come up against some pretty terrible situations.

JAN: You got that right.

RON: But we have to keep trying.

JAN: I'm not sure I can anymore.

RON: I know you can.

JAN: Don't be so sure.

RON: Hey, some day another little kid like that girl you just lost is going to be wheeled in here. Shot or stabbed. Beat or abused by her parents or some maniac. Or maybe some little boy or little girl who was hit by some drunk will be rushed here. And he or she is going to need you. Someone who cares about him or her. *(He looks at her; she is thinking, then:)* You know what makes you a good doctor, Jan?

JAN: *(Being ironic)* Yeah, that diploma I got from Harvard Medical School. Right?

RON: No. Not some piece of paper hanging on some office wall. What makes you a good doctor is not taking that doll out of that little girl's hand tonight. You knew it was important to her. You knew that that doll had to be in that little hand. And you left it there. That is what makes you a good doctor and that is why I want you here on my staff. I don't want you chickening out on me, Jan — or on them.

JAN: But it all seems so hopeless. They just keep coming in here day and night, night and day. It's after midnight and they are still coming in. All that blood and humanity. And her. It just seems so overwhelming at times.

RON: *(Shrugs)* So?

JAN: So? Doesn't it bother you? The senselessness of it all?

RON: If there is one thing I've learned while being a doctor in this crazy city's emergency room, it's that if you don't let things that you can't change bother you, you'll be OK. It's not your fault that that little girl died. You did what you could for her. That's our job.

JAN: This is not just a job.

RON: You know what I mean, Janet. You just do the best you can do, and let the chips fall where they may.

JAN: Great philosophy.

RON: *(Shrugs)* I went to Harvard, too, but it's the only philosophy I have. So are you going to come back and do what you do best, or are you going to run away and let someone else take care of the next little girl they wheel in here, someone who may not care as much about her as I know you will? What's it going to be, doctor? *(Just then the hospital intercom blares the following and JAN and RON stop to listen to it.)*

VOICE OVER INTERCOM: Dr. Janet Rosen! Emergency in trauma room four! Stat!

RON: So what are you going to do, Dr. Rosen?

JAN: *(Thinks, then)* I guess the best I can do.

RON: Right. Come on. Someone needs you. *(They rush off as curtain falls.)*

The Employment Agent

PRODUCTION NOTES

PLAYERS: 2 players. They can be males or females.

PLAYING TIME: 7 minutes.

COSTUMES: MIME in leotard. AGENT in business suit.

PROPERTIES: Files, pad, pencil.

SOUND EFFECTS: Sound of typewriter bell.

The Employment Agent

CHARACTERS: AGENT, Acme Employment Agency worker; MIME, looking for work.

TIME: Today.

SETTING: A desk Left Center Stage with papers and file folders piled high on it. Chair behind and in front of desk. Filing cabinets on right of stage. Employment posters on wall. Backstage Center hangs sign ACME EMPLOYMENT AGENCY — ANY JOB FOR ANYBODY.

AT RISE: AGENT enters juggling file folders and trying not to drop them. Then straightens out piles of papers and file folders on desk.

AGENT: Look at all these files! Everyone wants a job. But not just any job. They all want a job that pays a fortune. Well, so do I. Why not? Hey, I'm smart! I'm a good worker. So why can't I have a great, high-paying job — one I really like? I sure didn't want this job. I wanted to be a famous baseball player. I almost made the team, too. I could run, hit, catch, and slide. I could even pitch! *(Winds up a pitch.)* I had an arm . . . but they didn't pick me. I wonder why. I could have been in the World Series this year, but *nooo*. They wouldn't hire me. Well, they'll be sorry someday! *(Looks at file folder.)* Look at this. *(Looking at one file folder)* A nuclear physicist! A woman. Eight degrees. A Ph.D in . . . something to do with atomic theory. And she won't settle for that great job I offered her . . . *(Turns page.)* the one at the McNugget Chicken and Sushi Fast Food Store. I can't believe it. I found that job for her myself. It pays five bucks an hour. But is she happy? *Nooo.* She wants to build nuclear reactors and atom smashers. Good luck, lady! *(Tosses her folder away and looks at another folder.)* Look at this guy. A brain surgeon. Twenty years experience at

New York University Hospital, five years at the Sorbonne in France. And was he happy when I offered him that great job washing cars at Wet Willie's Wash and Blow Dry Custom Car Care Center? Nope. *(Yells)* **Ingrate! Some people are never satisfied! And that job paid four bucks an hour — and tips to boot! And all the cold showers you could take.** *(Tosses file on desk.)* **No one is happy. Everyone wants the world's greatest job and me to get it for them. Well, I'm sorry. OK? I can't even get the job I want. Me — who wanted to play major league baseball. Would they hire me? No.** *(Looks at file folder.)* **Look at this. That last woman that was in here. A woman with five kids. She just wanted a baby sitting job. I asked her, lady, what experience do you have baby sitting? And she looks at me like I'm an idiot. Give me a break. So I get her this great job. True, it has nothing to do with baby sitting. But it paid well. Was she happy with that job I got her? No. Beats me why. She'll make a bundle doing it. I mean all she has to do is paint the Brooklyn Bridge! OK, OK — so it needs two coats. Not that difficult in the winter. The paint dries faster; the job pays well. So what's a few blizzards?** *(Shrugs)* **But would she take it?** *Nooo.* *(Sits behind desk.)* **Time for another job seeker. Wonderful. Next!** *(In walks MIME. AGENT is surprised and a bit shocked. AGENT tentatively puts out hand to shake.)* **Ah, er . . . hello.**

MIME: *(Shakes AGENT's hand quickly.)*

AGENT: Have a seat.

MIME: *(Mimes sitting down on invisible chair, but AGENT runs and quickly gets MIME a chair.)*

AGENT: There. That's better. Now I assume you are looking for a job. Is that correct?

MIME: *(Nods and looks proudly at AGENT.)*

AGENT: Wonderful. OK. *(Takes out a pad.)* **First I have to ask you a few questions.**

MIME: *(Mimes, "Sure, go ahead. I'm all ears.")*

AGENT: I think you're trying to tell me to go ahead. You're all ears. Is that it?

MIME: *(Nods)*

AGENT: Good, good. Great. Right. First question. Name?

MIME: *(Uses mime and charades to tell AGENT MIME's name is Sandy Winters.)*

AGENT: Er . . . beach . . . no . . . sand?

MIME: *(Nods, but mimes AGENT is close, but needs to say more.)*

AGENT: Sandy!

MIME: *(Nods rapidly.)*

AGENT: OK. Sandy . . . storm . . . wind . . . winter . . . Winters!

MIME: *(Nods)*

AGENT: Great. Your name is Sandy Winters. Can you read, Sandy?

MIME: *(Mimes taking out a very big and heavy book, putting on glasses and reading book.)*

AGENT: Yes. Can read, wears glasses. *(Peeks at glasses.)* Bifocals, I believe. Excellent. Next question: can you write?

MIME: *(Mimes taking out a quill pen; feather tickles MIME's nose.)*

AGENT: A quill pen. Feather tickles your nose. Wonderful.

MIME: *(Mimes writing on a note pad.)*

AGENT: Excellent. You can read and you can write. Ahhh, but can you type?

MIME: *(Mimes typing away very fast, suddenly a bell goes off and AGENT jumps.)*

AGENT: Terrific! Now please don't take offense to my next question, but I must ask it. You won't be offended or hurt?

MIME: *(Shakes head as if to say, "no, don't worry.")*

AGENT: Good. I wouldn't want to hurt a mime's feelings. OK. Here's the big one. Can you . . . er . . . speak?

MIME: *(Quickly nods and stands. Mimes giving a speech to a large audience, but nothing comes out of MIME's mouth.)*

AGENT: Ah-ha. I see. Great. *(Makes a note on pad.)* Can . . . um . . . speak. *(Puts on a big smile for the MIME.)* Excellent. Well, you certainly have many skills. There is one more

question, however.

MIME: *(Mimes, "I'm ready, fire away.")*

AGENT: **OK. Can you sing?**

MIME: *(Nods happily and breaks into a silent song.)*

AGENT: **Ah, grand opera! Rigoletto, I believe. Wonderful, but not exactly what I had in mime — I mean mind. Nevertheless, you'll be perfect for this job.** *(Sinisterly)* **Just perfect.** *(Smiles slyly and laughs silently but fiendishly. MIME is happy and sits and waits attentively for new job as AGENT goes to filing cabinet and pulls out a file. He gets phone number from file, dials it, then speaks.)* **Booking Central? Jerry Glitz here. Great news. Got just the right man for the big one. OK? Right! Bye.** *(AGENT turns again to the MIME.)* **You're going to sing "The Star Spangled Banner" at the opening game of the World Series** *(Ironically)* **— for my ... er ... favorite team.** *(AGENT obviously hates that team.)*

MIME: *(Ecstatic over getting the job. MIME jumps up, shakes AGENT's hand hardily and rapidly, and starts to exit, happily practicing silent singing. AGENT aside to audience)*

AGENT: **Boy, is that baseball team going to be surprised! A silent singer. A mime to sing the National Anthem!** *(Giggles)* **They're going to go bananas! Good. That's what they get for not hiring me! OK! Now, let them squirm!** *(To MIME)* **I hope they love the way you sing!**

MIME: **So do I! I've been a mime for so long I almost forgot I could sing!** *(Suddenly MIME bursts into beautiful rendition of "Star Spangled Banner." AGENT is shocked and collapses onto floor as MIME exits singing.)*

Buried Alive

PRODUCTION NOTES

PLAYERS: 2 males.

PLAYING TIME: About 10 minutes.

COSTUMES: Dusty overalls, work boots, miners' helmets with lights on them. The light on ROY's helmet is broken and out.

PROPERTIES: 2 flashlights.

LIGHTING EFFECTS: The stage is bathed in a coal blue light. The only apparent light should come from the men's flashlights.

SOUND EFFECTS: Loud sound of cave-in. Dripping water, very faint sound of digging.

Buried Alive

CHARACTERS: TIM, an older miner; ROY, a young, new miner.

TIME: Today.

SETTING: Deep in a coal mine, dust and rubble everywhere.

AT RISE: Darkness and loud sound of a cave-in. TIM and ROY are getting to their feet. They are holding flashlights. ROY's helmet light is broken.

TIM: *(Getting up from rubble)* **Are you all right, Roy?**

ROY: *(As they dust themselves off)* **Yeah.** *(Looking around)* **I think so. Are we trapped? Are we?**

TIM: **There was a cave-in.**

ROY: **I know that. Are we trapped?** *(TIM looks around.)* **We're trapped. There's no way out. We're trapped. How deep are we?**

TIM: **A mile.**

ROY: **A mile! They'll never find us.**

TIM: **Relax, Roy.**

ROY: **Relax? Man, we're dead. Dead. I knew I shouldn't have taken this job. I've always hated this mine. It killed my father. Now it's going to kill me.**

TIM: *(Looking around)* **We don't know that yet. There may still be a way out. Come on. Help me. Let's look around.** *(TIM looks into left wing, then right wing.)* **Come on, Roy. Don't just stand there.**

ROY: **It's no use. Once these mines go, it's all over. Soon we'll run out of air. Or the gas will get us.** *(Sniffs air.)* **You smell any gas?**

TIM: **No. Look around. Tell me if you feel a draft coming in or see any light.**

ROY: *(Looking around)* **I'll look. But once we run out of air, it will be a slow death from suffocation.** *(Stops looking around and begins to pace frantically.)* **I don't want to die. I**

don't want to die!

TIM: Shut up! All right? Shut up and help me! There could still be a way out of this.

ROY: No there isn't. We're dead. Dead. *(ROY sits down.)* We'll suffocate and die, buried alive.

TIM: *(Goes over to ROY.)* Get up.

ROY: No.

TIM: I said, get up!

ROY: Why? What's the use? We're dead.

TIM: *(Grabs ROY by lapels and pulls him up.)* Get up! Get up! Get up!

ROY: *(Stands, then trying to break free)* I'm up! I'm up! *(Breaks free.)* But we're dead! And you know it.

TIM: No, I do not. We're not dead. And we're going to get out of here. You hear me, Roy? *(ROY calms down.)* We're going to get out of here. OK? *(ROY nods.)* OK. So help me look around. There still might be a way out of here. *(They look around.)*

ROY: There's no way out. There never is from these death traps. These old mines. There's nothing here but shoring and rubble. We don't even have lights. Once these batteries go, we'll be in the dark.

TIM: We could be rescued by then. They know where we are. They'll find us.

ROY: Yeah. They'll find us. They'll find us dead.

TIM: *(Giving up the search for a way out)* They'll find us. And we'll be alive when they do.

ROY: *(Giving up the search for a way out)* There's no way out. See? You couldn't find one. You couldn't find a way out, and neither could I. See? I told you. We're trapped. Trapped a mile below the surface with the rats and the gas. I'll never see my wife and kid again.

TIM: You have a kid?

ROY: Yeah. A little boy. Maggie and me just had him. He's only a month old. That's why I'm down here. We needed the money. I didn't want to work in the mine. After my daddy died down here, I swore never to come down here.

TIM: But you needed the money.

ROY: Right. And now Maggie will be left all alone with the kid. *(Paces)* She'll never make it. She needs me.

TIM: Hey, Roy, we're going to get out of here. I've been in a few of these cave-ins before. They seem hopeless at first, all the dust and rubble. The darkness. It can really shake you up. No matter how tough you are, you get trapped in one of these mines and you feel buried alive, helpless. It can really wreck your nerves.

ROY: Yeah, really. How long you been working in these mines?

TIM: All my life. Since I was old enough to dig, to hold a shovel. My whole family's worked in this mine. Coal is a family tradition, you could say.

ROY: Some tradition.

TIM: It's all we were able to do. My granddaddy and daddy were dirt poor. They both started working here as kids. It was all they ever knew. All I know.

ROY: I hate it. I never liked the mines. There's something terrifying about going deep into the earth. I'm not claustrophobic, but I don't like being trapped. *(Walks around.)* I like my freedom. I don't like to be trapped. *(TIM sees that ROY is about to panic.)* I hate being trapped. I want to get out of here. Now! Fast!

TIM: *(Stops ROY from pacing.)* Hey! Roy! Relax, man. Sit down. Catch your breath. We'll get out of here. Trust me. OK? It just seems bad at first. But I guarantee you, help is on the way.

ROY: *(Listens)* Yeah? You hear anything? I sure don't. All I hear is dripping water, and us. No one is going to rescue us. I'll never see my family again.

TIM: Yes you will. Roy, tell me more about Maggie. How'd you meet her?

ROY: Why? Is this keep-Roy-talking time? Keep him talking so he won't panic? Is that it?

TIM: Roy, you keep talking, you don't panic. You don't panic, you survive. So talk, OK? Tell me about Maggie. How'd you meet her? Is she pretty?

ROY: She's sort of pretty.

TIM: Sort of? You tell Maggie that?

ROY: No. I just mean she's not — you know — like one of those Playboy types. She's sort of . . . plain. But to me she's beautiful. She's got this way about her. A quietness.

TIM: What is she? A mouse?

ROY: No way. Not Maggie. When she has something to say, she says it. She won't let anyone push her around. But she's not mean. She's just . . . she has this sweetness about her. I don't know. All I know is when I see her, something in me jumps. It's like this light goes on. Nothing can hurt me, I can do anything. Like work down here. I'm doing it for Maggie. If it was up to me, I'd be a beach bum in California or Hawaii.

TIM: No, you wouldn't. If you were a bum, you wouldn't be here shoveling this stuff for Maggie and your kid. It's funny what we do for those we love. Love is funny. It can turn people around. It can make a wimp into a man and a man into a silly kid.

ROY: Yeah. When I met Maggie, it was like I was a little crazy. I started brushing my teeth a couple of more times a day, shaving twice a day, taking a lot of extra showers, and not all cold showers.

TIM: But a few.

ROY: Yeah, right. A few. My mom said, "Roy, what's wrong with you? You sick, boy?"

TIM: Lovesick.

ROY: I guess so. Maggie turned me around. I used to hang out, didn't care about anything. Then I met Maggie. I finally found something worth working for, doing things for, changing. You know?

TIM: Women'll do that to ya.

ROY: Yeah. Before I met her, nothing seemed to matter. It was like I didn't care what I was, what I looked like. Nothing.

TIM: I know what you're saying. Like I said, women can do that to ya. Seems like they're the missing link. The part of us that gives it all meaning. You go through life wondering, what does all this mean? Why am I here? Then one day you meet some girl and it hits you. That is why. She is the reason you are here. All of a sudden you have something that gives your life some direction, some meaning.

ROY: Yeah. When we started dating, I wanted to take her everywhere. All the places I was to when I was a kid. The state fair, the zoo. I wanted her to know everything I knew. It's like I wanted her to be a part of me.

TIM: They do grow on you.

ROY: Really. *(Thinks)* I wanted to tell her everything about my life. It's not that I wanted to change her or anything. I didn't.

TIM: I hear you.

ROY: I'd never want to change Maggie. I mean, I was attracted to her because of the way she was. Sure, when you first see them, all you see is the body. What they look like. On the surface. But that doesn't last. There's always going to be someone else who's going to look better. But Maggie was different.

TIM: That difference is what hooks you.

ROY: I guess so. Maggie was not as pretty as some girls I've been with, but she was different. There was something there besides a body. She liked to talk to me. We never got tired of each other. We thought we did a few times, but we couldn't quite forget about each other. She'd call me up just to talk, or I'd call her up. Finally, we realized that we were in love. You think love is seeing a pretty body, being attracted to some great looking woman. But that's not love. That's just the hormones. Love is different. It's something that grows on you.

TIM: Sort of creeps up on you.

ROY: Exactly. Little by little. It's like the bonds between you grow more and more, tighter and tighter. Then one day you realize you just can't live without this person. You don't care what she looks like so much. You care about how you feel when you're with her, when you're together. She just does something to you. Maggie is like that. I look at her and I think, I can do anything now. Anything for her. Anything for us.

TIM: And now you got the kid.

ROY: Yeah. And he will never work in this mine. Never. He's going to college. He's going to be an astronaut. It's going to be the stars for him, not some hellhole a mile underground. Never.

TIM: What does Maggie say?

ROY: She wants to have a lot of kids. And she wants to move away from here. She wants us to find a nice place to raise the kids, a farm maybe. Or a little place in the country. Away from the mines. That's why she took that job in the mine's office. We're saving so we can get out of here one day. But now all that may be over.

TIM: It ain't over yet. It never is over till you're six feet under.

ROY: Or five thousand. Accept it, Tim, we're dead.

TIM: No, we aren't. Think positive, man. I got out of these cave-ins before, and I'll do it again. And so will you. I'm your lucky charm. I'm a survivor and soon you'll be one too. You'll have some story to tell your grandkids, Roy boy. You'll see.

ROY: I wish I could be more like you. You're so calm. Aren't you afraid?

TIM: *(Looking up)* Listen. You hear that?

ROY: *(Listens)* I don't hear anything. Just that water dripping.

TIM: *(Listens)* I sure thought I heard digging.

ROY: You're hearing things. No one is digging. No one even knows we're trapped down here. Buried alive like a couple of rats. I don't want to die like a rat. Not now. I have a family. They need me. Do you have a family?

TIM: A wife and two kids.

ROY: Aren't you afraid you'll never see them again?

TIM: I try not to think of that. But you have this tendency to keep reminding me.

ROY: Sorry. But that's how I feel. Trapped. *(Yells up to ceiling.)* Do you hear me? We're trapped! Get us out of here!

TIM: Hey, careful you don't start another cave-in. Calm down, OK?

ROY: I wish I could be like you. Calm. Like nothing is wrong. How do you do it? How do you keep from thinking we're buried alive?

TIM: I try not to think of that.

ROY: So what do you think of?

TIM: I'll tell you what I don't think of. I don't think of being buried alive. Or being a mile deep. Don't do that. Try to think of us being just beneath the surface.

ROY: Just beneath the surface?

TIM: Right. In ways we all are. That's where most of us live. Hiding out just beneath the surface. People only seem to see the surface details of each other. Never what is just beneath the surface.

ROY: So what are you talking about? You telling me they'll never find us *(Sarcastically)* just beneath the surface? Is that what you're getting at?

TIM: No. I just mean it's like you and Maggie. Most other guys just saw her surface features. Maybe they didn't see her real beauty, like you did, underneath. Know what I mean?

ROY: I think the coal gas is getting to you. I don't know what you're talking about. All I know is we're never going to get out of here. I'm never going to see Maggie again or my kid. No one is coming to get us out. No one knows we're even trapped down here.

TIM: You got to learn to think more positive, Roy boy. You are way too negative for a miner.

ROY: I hate this mine. I hate all mines. Man wasn't meant to be a miner. This is no place for anyone. Rats belong down here. Moles. But not people. Not us! *(Hears something.)* Wait a minute. You hear that?

TIM: *(Listens)* I think I do. Yeah. Just maybe. Very faint. Hear it?

ROY: *(Listening)* Yeah. You think it's them?

TIM: What do you think?

ROY: It sounds like it might be them.

TIM: It might be them tunneling in from the shaft next to this one.

ROY: *(Listening to the rear wall)* Yeah. I think I hear digging. It's them! They're coming to get us! I just know they are!

TIM: Now you're thinking like a miner. *(They sit down and wait.)* Now you're thinking positive.

ROY: I'm trying, man. I'm trying.

TIM: You're doing just fine. *(Curtain falls.)* You're a miner now, Roy boy. *(Curtain)*

The Breakup

PRODUCTION NOTES

PLAYERS: 1 male; 1 female.

PLAYING TIME: About 10 minutes.

COSTUMES: BEN in business suit, DONNA in jeans and pretty blouse.

PROPERTIES: Woman's wedding ring.

SOUND EFFECTS: Door closing.

The Breakup

CHARACTERS: BEN; DONNA, Ben's wife.

TIME: Evening.

SETTING: The living room of BEN and DONNA's home. A sofa
Stage Center. An easy chair on left, reading light on right. A
large frame with many family photos hangs on backdrop.

AT RISE: BEN and DONNA sit on sofa, as far apart as possible.

DONNA: *(Looks up, shakes her head, then:)* **I'm really sorry you
feel that way, Ben.**

BEN: **Look, I'm sorry. What more can I tell you? I'm sorry, I'm
sorry, I'm sorry. But that's the way it is.**

DONNA: **I guess so.**

BEN: **It is. I'm sorry.**

DONNA: **You said that already.**

BEN: **I'm sorry.**

DONNA: **I get the picture.**

BEN: **It's just the way it is. The way things happen.**

DONNA: **These things don't just happen.**

BEN: **It just happened, OK, Donna? What do you want me to
say? I'm sorry. OK? I'm sorry.**

DONNA: *(Looking him in the face)* **What about the kids? What
are we going to tell them?**

BEN: *(He gets up and walks around, looking at family photos.)* **I
don't know. I don't know.**

DONNA: *(She gets up and walks to him and they look at family
photos.)* **Well, we'll have to tell them something. They'll
want to know what's going to happen to them.**

BEN: *(Looking at her, then walks away)* **Nothing is going to
happen to them. Nothing.**

DONNA: **Nothing? Their whole life is going to be torn apart
by this. They are going to want to know why you don't
love me anymore, why *we* don't love each other anymore.**

They are going to want to know where they are going to
live, with me or with you. They are going to want to know
where they are going to go to school. If you still love them.

BEN: Of course I still love them.

DONNA: You have an odd way of showing it. This is going to
hurt them. They are going to be scared. Kids are easily
frightened when their parents fight.

BEN: I'm not fighting with you.

DONNA: You know what I mean. They are going to feel very
insecure.

BEN: I promise you, I will try to make this easy for you and
them. You can keep everything. The car. The house. The
kids. They are going to live right here with you. I'm not
going to fight you over this, or over them. I'll be sure all
the bills get paid. You'll be fine. You all will. The last
thing you or they need is a fight. The kids don't need that.
So you'll all stay right here. You can have everything —
even the kids. OK?

DONNA: They love you too, you know. You can't just say I
can have them. And what about me? Us? I can't believe
you did this to me, to us. Why? Are you tired of me? Am
I not enough for you? What did I do wrong? What? What
did I do wrong?

BEN: Donna, come on. You didn't do anything wrong.

DONNA: Oh. So then you're the rat. This is all your fault.

BEN: Yes. It's all my fault.

DONNA: But why? We were so happy. At least I thought we
were. Maybe *I* was just happy. You were just acting. Is
that it? Were you just acting? Were you really miserable
all this while?

BEN: Yes. *(Then)* No.

DONNA: Yes? No? You were and you weren't? Or you were
happy but you weren't acting? Or you weren't acting, you
were just unhappy? Or happy? What is it?! You were or
weren't happy? You can tell me. I'm your wife. At least for

now.

BEN: I was happy, with her. But unhappy about you and the kids.

DONNA: Great. So what is she? Younger? Prettier? More exciting? *(She waits for an answer.)* What's wrong, Benjamin? Cat got your tongue? Oh, excuse the pun.

BEN: Look. I'm sorry —

DONNA: You're sorry? I'm sorry! Sorry I married you, you bum! How could you do this to me? To the kids! I can't believe this. But you know, I sensed something was wrong. You did seem cooler, but I figured you were just going through some bad times at the office.

BEN: I was. That's part of the problem.

DONNA: It was? Why didn't you tell me? You always told me when you had a problem. *(Looks at him, then away.)* Oh, I see. You were letting her hold your hand. *(Looks at him.)* Is that it? You were telling her instead of me?

BEN: Yes. *(DONNA shakes her head and sits in easy chair.)* She was right there for me.

DONNA: And where was I? On the moon?

BEN: You know what I mean.

DONNA: *(Gets up and walks around.)* I just don't know what we're going to tell the kids.

BEN: We'll tell them it's not their fault. This just happened. They will be fine. We're still their parents. That has not changed.

DONNA: That all sounds so pat. But they're little kids. They're going to think they did something wrong. That's how kids are. They see things from a whole different viewpoint.

BEN: We'll sit with them. We'll explain it. We'll tell them we love them very much and that this is just between their mommy and daddy and we both still love them. They'll understand.

DONNA: *(Looks at him.)* And what are you going to tell me?

BEN: *(Looks away from her.)* I told you I was sorry.

DONNA: You're not going to get off that easy.

BEN: Donna, you don't have to threaten me. You can have everything: the house, the kids.

DONNA: I'm not talking about that! I'm talking about us, our life together, till death do us part. Remember that promise you made to me; we made to each other? Or have you forgotten it?

BEN: I haven't forgotten.

DONNA: Good. And I hope you haven't forgotten all the dreams we had. Our house. Our kids.

BEN: You've got all those things.

DONNA: Things? Your children are not things. I didn't want things. I wanted *us*. I wanted *our* kids. They are little lives *we* brought into this world. *(She laughs ironically.)* They are supposed to be symbols of our love.

BEN: They are. I still love you. Why do you think I told you about her? I had to be honest with you.

DONNA: *(Sarcastically)* Thank you for your honesty. It's just what I needed.

BEN: You wanted me to lie to you? To tell you I don't love her? To tell you I just had a fling?

DONNA: No. I wanted you to be my husband. Be faithful to me. Be the one who loves *me*, not some other woman. That's the kind of honesty I wanted from you. *(BEN looks down, having nothing to say.)* You have nothing to say now? I just hope you can be honest with the kids. Because they still love you.

BEN: And you don't?

DONNA: Me? Right now I hate your guts. To me you are the lowest of the low. I'd like to rip your heart out, because you just ripped mine out.

BEN: I'm a rat. What can I tell you?

DONNA: Are you sure this isn't just some little fling? She just caught your eye? She was standing in just the right light?

BEN: No. I love her. And I still love you. I love you both.

DONNA: Well, you can't have us both. That's not the way it is. You're not some kid anymore out looking for *(Makes quote sign in his face)* "love." You're a big boy now, a married man, an adult. You have to choose. You have to pick someone you really love, not just because she looks good in the right light, but because you love her for the way she is. We have a whole history together, Ben. You always said I'd make a great mother. Is that the problem? You're tired of me being a mommy and you being a daddy? You want to become some kid again? Chasing girls? Is that it?

BEN: I don't know what I want anymore. I love you, I love the kids, I love her.

DONNA: Are you going to marry her?

BEN: Yes. If she'll have me.

DONNA: For your sake I hope she will, because you are out of here, Benjamin. You are out of here for good. You can take your toothbrush and your rechargeable electric shaver and get out of this house! Get out of here!

BEN: Donna, come on, you'll wake the kids.

DONNA: Oh, excuse me. I'll let them sleep. I'll tell them all about this tomorrow. Tomorrow is another day. By the way, Ben, you won't be here. So do you have any suggestions on how I should break the news to them? How I should tell them their daddy is a two-faced rat who cheated on their mommy and walked out on them? What should I say? Daddy will write. He'll call ya. Be sure the answering machine is on. What should I tell the kids, you rat?!

BEN: Look, I'll stay the night.

DONNA: No! I want you out of here.

BEN: I'll sleep on the sofa. Then I can be with you in the morning. We can tell the kids together. *(DONNA thinks.)* OK?

DONNA: I don't know what to think. Right now I'm so mad, I don't know what to think.

BEN: It'll be better if we tell them together.

– 73 –

DONNA: Sure. Then you'll pack up and walk out on them.

BEN: I am not walking out on them.

DONNA: Yes you are. You think they want this? They want you here. They love you. You're their father. You're supposed to help them put their toys together, set up the trains at Christmas, take them camping.

BEN: I'll still do that.

DONNA: When? On weekends, with her? They'll love that.

BEN: I know you must hate her now.

DONNA: It's you I hate. Her I don't even know. But to be honest, if she were a nun, right now I'd hate her guts.

BEN: It's not her fault. She didn't even know I was married.

DONNA: Does she now? *(BEN looks down.)* She doesn't?

BEN: Not yet.

DONNA: Wonderful. You're being honest with her, too, I see. You know, Ben, honesty is not one of your strong points.

BEN: Tell me about it. I feel real bad about all this. I didn't mean to screw everything up. Maybe I'm going through something.

DONNA: Yeah. You're going through a divorce.

BEN: I promise you, Donna, I won't fight you on this. You can have everything. And I am sorry. I never meant to hurt anyone. These things just happen.

DONNA: No they don't! Be honest. They need a little help to happen. You just let it happen. You were too weak to stop it from happening. I really don't care if you seduced her or she seduced you. It's not her fault. It's your fault. You were the one who was married. You should have let her know before it went too far. Look, Ben, I work in an office too, you know. Guys come on to me all the time. All I have to do is flash my wedding ring in their face. *(She flashes her wedding ring in his face.)* See it? It works every time. You should try it sometime. *(Struggles to take off her ring and does. She hands it to him.)* Here. Something to remember me by. Now please leave.

BEN: *(Hands her back the ring.)* **You sure you don't want me to be here tomorrow with you when you tell the kids?**

DONNA: All I know is I want you out of here right now. Out. OK? You got that? Or do I have to spell it out for you: O-U-T — out. Please.

BEN: OK. But I'm sorry.

DONNA: *(Sits on sofa.)* So am I.

BEN: I'll call you.

DONNA: Right.

BEN: Bye, Donna.

DONNA: Yeah, bye.

BEN: I love you.

DONNA: Sure you do. *(BEN exits and we hear a door slam as DONNA sits alone looking at her wedding ring as curtain falls.)*

You Live and Learn

PLAYERS: 2 males.

PLAYING TIME: About 10 minutes.

COSTUMES: Jeans, sneakers, similar shirts. Maybe even similar sunglasses. They both wear similar carved leather belts.

PROPERTIES: Electric guitar.

SOUND EFFECTS: Loud rock and roll music that MAN mimes playing.

NOTE: MAN and BOY are the same person, so their mannerisms should be the same.

You Live and Learn

CHARACTERS: MAN, BOY.

TIME: Night.
SETTING: An empty stage, as if under starry sky at night.
AT RISE: MAN enters from left; BOY enters from right. There is a definite similarity between them.

MAN: **Hello.**

BOY: *(Backs away a bit)* **My mother told me never to talk to strangers.**

MAN: **Yes. You're right. Very good advice. But aren't you out very late for someone your age?**

BOY: **Maybe. Maybe not.**

MAN: **I see.** *(Looking up into the sky)* **Well . . . it is a nice night.**

BOY: **Yes.** *(Looking up)* **Look at all those stars.**

MAN: **It's like a dream.**

BOY: **Exactly what I was thinking.**

MAN: **I used to love sitting out in my backyard at night as a boy, looking up at the stars.**

BOY: **Yes.** *(They look at each other, then up into sky.)* **I do that too.**

MAN: *(Looking up)* **There's Orion and Cassiopeia — and look at how bright Vega is.**

BOY: **A star of the first magnitude. Like I'm going to be when I get older.**

MAN: **Yes. As a boy, I had hopes and dreams that I was going to be a star when I grew up. A rock star.** *(Walks to other side of stage, alone.)* **At least that's what I thought I would be when I grew up, but you live and learn.**

BOY: **I don't know about that. But I do know I'm going to be a rock star when I'm older.**

MAN: **You too, eh?**

BOY: **Yes. I love music.**

MAN: **So do I. In fact, I'm a professor of musicology over at**

the university.

BOY: *(Not impressed)* Oh, yeah?

MAN: Not impressed, eh?

BOY: It sounds sort of boring. Now you take being a rock star. Now that's exciting. Look out Elvis and Mick, here I come!

MAN: You sound just like me when I was your age. I had this great dream of becoming a rock star, one all the girls would go crazy over —

BOY: Yeah! Like me. I'm going to be famous. All the girls are going to be begging to meet me. I'll have to get a couple of big strong bodyguards to beat them off. *(He laughs.)* Maybe. You know what I mean?

MAN: I sure do. I used to think just like you. So what instrument do you play?

BOY: I play a few.

MAN: Great. So do I. Which ones do you play?

BOY: The usual: keyboard, guitar, drums, a little sax.

MAN: Yeah! So do I. You like to practice?

BOY: No.

MAN: Neither did I when I was your age, but you really have to practice if you want to make it big on the music scene. There's a lot of competition out there.

BOY: I know. I look at TV and see Mick and Elvis and Paul and Jon Bon Jovi, and I think . . . can I ever be as good as they are?

MAN: You mean as good as they were.

BOY: No. I mean as good as they are. They will never die. Rock and roll is here to stay.

MAN: Yeah. Right. I know how you feel. Elvis, Mick, Paul, Jon — they are the best. It's pretty hard these days to get as far as they got.

BOY: Yeah. Hey, you're a pretty cool guy for a professor. Most guys like you, I thought, were real dull. But you seem cool.

MAN: Hey, kid, I was like you once. And part of me still is. Sure, you live and you learn about life and such. You grow up. *(A little sad)* And you finally let your dream of being a rock star go, and you just settle down. You settle for a good job and a house and a good wife, and two or three healthy kids, a white picket fence and two cars. You just settle.

BOY: Not me. I'll never just settle. I'll never give up my dream. Never.

MAN: Who said anything about giving up?

BOY: I thought you did.

MAN: No. I just said I decided that what I really wanted was a happy life, doing what I love — music — but not just beating my brains out trying to be another Elvis.

BOY: There'll never be another Elvis.

MAN: Right. There was only one Elvis. So we just grow up and do the best we can with what we have.

BOY: You mean give up being a rock star for a job teaching music at a local college?

MAN: If it makes you happy.

BOY: Does it make you happy?

MAN: Sure it does. I get the best of all possible worlds.

BOY: Like what?

MAN: I get just what I really always wanted: a wonderful woman who loves me, great kids, and a job in music. And I actually get paid fairly well for it too.

BOY: Not as well as a rock star.

MAN: No. True. But then I don't have to spend my life on the road going from one motel to the next. That can be pretty lonely.

BOY: Not with all those cute groupies.

MAN: I don't know. I'm happy with the way things turned out.

BOY: I guess you are. But I'm going to give being a rock star my best shot.

MAN: Right. Do it. Try as hard as you can, practice as hard as you can, listen to all the musicians you like. And hang in there. Take a chance. Take your best shot. If you really want to be a rock star, you'll get there. Maybe you won't be another Elvis or Mick, but you'll be the best you can be. Maybe someone will be saying they want to be like you one day.

BOY: Does anyone ever say that to you, that they want to be as good as you?

MAN: Sure. My students think I'm terrific. And that makes me feel good, like I'm making a difference. Hey, who knows. Maybe one day one of my students will be a rock star.

BOY: Yeah. Maybe. So what are you doing out this late?

MAN: Dreaming, I think. I do it nearly every night.

BOY: Dream?

MAN: Yes. Don't you?

BOY: Sure. So what do you dream about?

MAN: My childhood. When I was young like you.

BOY: Really? What was it like when you were young like me?

MAN: All the kids wanted to be rock stars. We'd beg our parents to let us take guitar lessons. Every kid wanted an electric guitar. And lessons.

BOY: I know. I did the same thing. I begged and begged until my parents finally gave in. They bought me my first guitar for my tenth birthday.

MAN: No kidding. So did mine.

BOY: Really?

MAN: Yes. They bought me this really great Fender℗.

BOY: Me too. I love it. I can pick songs out by ear. You know, right off the radio.

MAN: I used to do that all the time.

BOY: Gee, you're a lot like me — even if you are an old guy.

MAN: Hey, I'm not that old. So you hate to practice too, eh?

BOY: Yep. Who needs to practice dumb scales when you can pick songs right out by ear?

MAN: Exactly. Er ... but from a professional point of view,

you really should practice.

BOY: I think I hear the professor talking now.

MAN: I guess you're right. But you know, sometimes I wonder if I had practiced just a little more, I might have made it. I just might have had that little edge you need to break into the big time. But I never did. I got close once, but here I am. Out stargazing, dreaming.

BOY: Like me. I often dream about being a rock star.

MAN: *(Looking at BOY, thinking, then)* Hey, do I know you?

BOY: No. Why?

MAN: You look so familiar.

BOY: *(Shrugs)* Well, OK, but I don't think we've ever met.

MAN: *(Points at him.)* Wait a minute. Now I know who you are.

BOY: You do? OK, I'll bite. Who am I?

MAN: You're me!

BOY: *(Backing away a bit as if frightened)* I'm . . . you?

MAN: Yes! Look. You're even wearing the leather belt I carved in my basement. Leather carving was my favorite hobby.

BOY: How did you know I carved this belt in my basement and that leather carving was my favorite hobby?

MAN: Because you're me! Now I know what's going on here. This is all a dream. We're dreaming — or rather I'm dreaming.

BOY: And I'm part of this dream?

MAN: No. You're me. I'm home in bed dreaming of my childhood, of what I wanted to be and what I finally became.

BOY: You're telling me, you're me as a man?

MAN: Yes!

BOY: Prove it.

MAN: OK. *(Pinches BOY.)* There. See?

BOY: I didn't feel a thing.

MAN: Of course you didn't. This is a dream. If it were real life, you'd have felt that pinch.

BOY: That's dumb. Maybe I'm just numb or something.

MAN: OK, then how about this little scar on my elbow? *(Shows BOY tiny scar.)* See? I bet you have one just like it.

BOY: I do.

MAN: You got it falling off your two-wheeler the day your dad — our dad, *my* dad — took off your training wheels.

BOY: *(Amazed, confused)* Yes. You're right.

MAN: See?

BOY: So then . . . I'm you?

MAN: Yes. So what do you think?

BOY: Well . . . you're . . . you're . . . OK, I guess.

MAN: You mean *you're* OK.

BOY: Yeah. I guess. So, I didn't practice enough, eh?

MAN: I guess not. But you are very happy. You have a great wife and three great kids.

BOY: Oh, yeah? Three kids, huh?

MAN: Yep.

BOY: What are their names?

MAN: Victor, Nicole and Jacqueline — in fact, Victor plays the drums.

BOY: No kidding!

MAN: No kidding. And his teacher says he's great!

BOY: All right! Hey, you know, suddenly I'm pretty happy.

MAN: Me too.

BOY: I like the way my life turned out. Maybe I'm not ever going to be a rock star, but I'm going to be OK. I'm going to be pretty happy.

MAN: You are. But, hey, it ain't over till it's over, as Yogi Berra says.

BOY: Yeah? So?

MAN: Wait, I'll show you. *(MAN runs off and gets his electric guitar.)* Check this out! *(As loud music plays, he mimes playing some really good rock and roll.)* How was that?

BOY: Fantastic! How did you learn to play like that?

MAN: One day I just started to practice.

BOY: You live and learn.

MAN: Right. You live and learn. *(Curtain as MAN plays rock and roll.)*

COMEDY SKETCHES

My Two Loves:
A Midsummer's Nightmare

PRODUCTION NOTES

PLAYERS: 3 females, 1 male.

PLAYING TIME: About 13 minutes.

COSTUMES: GARY in pajamas, ELLIE in bikini, LISA in very old-fashioned dress, TINA in body stocking with white diaphanous fabric over it.

PROPERTIES: Baseball cap.

My Two Loves:
A Midsummer's Nightmare

CHARACTERS: GARY, ELLIE, LISA, TINA.

TIME: Midsummer. Midnight.

SETTING: An empty stage, except for bed Rear Center Stage. This is taking place in GARY's mind. It is a dream.

AT RISE: GARY in pajamas tosses and turns in bed. He suddenly sits up as if frightened. He gets up and walks around, trying to think, trying to get his thoughts together.

GARY: *(Rubs his eyes.)* **What am I? Dreaming? I thought I was at home in bed dreaming about Ellie and Lisa.** *(To audience)* **This is all a dream, right? I know, I'll pinch myself.** *(Pinches himself.)* **Ouch. Maybe I'm not dreaming. All I know is I was in bed dreaming this really great dream about Ellie and Lisa.** *(Scratches his head.)* **Or was it a nightmare? Anyway, Lisa and Ellie are my girl friends. Yeah, I know, I know. I should have only one girl friend at a time. Well, just one close one anyhow. I know I should try to make up my mind and pick either Lisa or Ellie. But I'm young. I'm foolish. So what the heck.** *(Thinks)* **No, it's just not right. Two girl friends, especially two as close to my heart as Lisa and Ellie, can't be right. Not at the same time. This is a nightmare.** *(Shrugs)* **What can I do? I love them both. Ellie is so outgoing. She loves to do everything, go everywhere. We have so much fun together. Then there's Lisa. She's so sweet and quiet. She likes to go to quiet places. She loves classical music, jazz, easy listening. True, these things bore me — well, not totally, only slightly, but enough. You know what I mean? Too much Beethoven and I get depressed. Ellie loves rock and roll — action. I do, too. But not all the time. And Ellie loves football. I hate football. I love baseball. Lisa loves**

hockey. I hate hockey. I love baseball. And they both hate baseball. But I love them both. I know, I know, I have to make up my mind. It's not right to deceive them. No, they don't know about each other.

ELLIE and LISA:　*(Enter from opposite sides of stage.)* **Oh, yes we do, you rat!**

GARY:　*(Surprised, looks at them.)* **It's you!** *(To audience)* **I told you this was a nightmare!** *(To ELLIE and LISA)* **You! And you?** *(As he backs away from them)*

ELLIE:　*(As they approach him threateningly)* **Right. Ellie.**

LISA:　**And Lisa.**

ELLIE and LISA:　*(Pointing at him as they approach him and he backs away.)* **And we know all about you, Gary.**

GARY:　**This must be a dream!** *(They back him up against bed, he falls in it and stands up on bed.)*

ELLIE:　**Wrong.**

GARY:　**Wrong?**

LISA:　**Right. Wrong.**

GARY:　**You're telling me this is not a dream?**

ELLIE:　**I am.**

LISA:　**We sure are. This is no dream.**

GARY:　**Then what is it?**

ELLIE and LISA:　**A nightmare!**

ELLIE:　**Yours!**

GARY:　**But what are you doing in it?**

LISA:　*(They walk away from bed and he comes down off it, but keeps a safe distance from them.)* **Hey, I'd much rather be in Tom Cruise's dream than in yours, you bum.**

ELLIE:　**Right. And I'd much rather be in Mick Jaggers' dream.**

LISA:　**But we're stuck with yours.**

ELLIE:　**What a drag.**

GARY:　**I'm sorry my dreams are so boring.**

LISA:　**Oh, they're not always.** *(Smiles, tries not to giggle.)*

ELLIE:　**No. They aren't always.** *(She and LISA laugh.)*

GARY: So you're not . . . jealous?

ELLIE and LISA: Of course we are!

ELLIE: Yeah. And who told you to dream about Madonna last night?

LISA: Or Debbie Gibson last Tuesday?!

ELLIE: Her, too?

LISA: Yes. And Princess Di. And even Fergie.

ELLIE: You cad!

LISA: Yeah, Gary. What's wrong with dreaming about just me? Huh?

ELLIE: Or me?

GARY: Look, I'm sorry. But when I'm asleep, I have no control over who I dream about.

LISA: That's what they all say.

GARY: But it's true. Really. Even Freud says so.

LISA: Freud? What about Jung?

ELLIE: Or Pee Wee Herman?

GARY and LISA: Who?

ELLIE: I was just kidding.

GARY: Oh. Well, as I was saying, it's true. My subconscious just takes over. But I am dreaming of you now.

ELLIE: Yeah. Great. The only problem is you're dreaming about *(Points to LISA)* her, too.

LISA: *(Points to ELLIE)* And her, too.

GARY: Yes! I hate it! OK? I'd much rather be dreaming of just one of you!

ELLIE and LISA: Which one?

ELLIE: Right. Which one?

LISA: You were dreaming about the both of us.

GARY: I have a problem. All right?

ELLIE: What problem, Gary?

LISA: Yeah, right. What's the problem, Gary? You can't make up your mind? Is that it?

ELLIE: A little indecisive?

LISA: Huh? That it, Gar?

GARY: Yes, Lisa. Sorry.

ELLIE: He's sorry.

GARY: I'm sorry, Ellie. What do you want me to say?

ELLIE: I want you to say you love me, just me. And not her!

LISA: No. You must say you love me. I'm the cute one. The quiet one. I love you. Our love is true love. Not just lust like with *(Points to ELLIE.)* her.

ELLIE: What? What do you mean? *(Hugs GARY; he pulls away.)* I love this guy! He makes me laugh. We go everywhere together. Hey, how did you get into this dream anyway, Lisa? You should be home in bed dreaming about Beethoven or some dead poet!

LISA: And what about you? You should be home dreaming about some dumb punk rocker or rapper or . . . or some dumb football jock. You don't belong in *(Points to GARY)* his head, in his subconscious! I do!

GARY: Hold it, OK? Let's just talk this over like three normal adults.

ELLIE: We are not adults!

LISA: Right! We are figments of your dumb imagination.

ELLIE: Your sordid imagination!

LISA: *(Looks down at herself.)* And look at me! I don't even look like this in real life! I'm much . . . er . . . heavier. Hey, I look pretty . . . slim.

GARY: No. That's how you always look. At least to me.

ELLIE: *(Looks at herself.)* Hey, wait a second here. Look at me. OK? Who took away my real figure? Where are my curves? Where are my big . . . er . . . *(Looks at GARY with her hands on her hips.)* What's going on here, Gary? Huh?

GARY: Ellie, I love you just like that. You look fine. To me you're beautiful — you're both beautiful. And that's the problem. I think I'm in love with you both.

ELLIE and LISA: Well, you can't be! It's not right!

GARY: Right? Right? What does any of this have to do with right? This is just a dream. A nightmare. It's not a matter of right or wrong. It's just the way I see this whole situation.

ELLIE: Well, wake up!

LISA: Yeah. Right! Wake up!

GARY: If I wake up, you'll both just disappear, vanish.

ELLIE: *(Scared, paces nervously)* Right, right. I forgot that. Don't wake up.

LISA: Please. Just relax. Sleep, sleep, sleep.

GARY: I am, I am. I guess what all this is about is us. My relationship with you. Our relationship. I guess it's true what they say.

ELLIE: True what who says?

LISA: Yeah. What are you talking about, Gary? I know my I.Q. is much higher than hers —

ELLIE: Thanks a lot, Lisa. You were always such a snob.

LISA: No, I'm not. And don't blame me for any of this. *(Points to GARY.)* It's all his fault. This is his dream. He's the one who thinks I'm the genius and you're the bimbo.

ELLIE: What?!

GARY: I never said that! Never, Ellie. I think you're a wonderful girl! Really!

ELLIE: Well, I'm no bimbo. Is it my fault that you conjured me up like this? This is not the real me, you know. All I can say is that I'm glad I have on my Sunday dress.

LISA: Er ... Ellie ... you have on a bikini. You must have missed that.

ELLIE: What?! *(Looks at herself, suddenly shy.) Gary!* You ... you ...

GARY: I'm sorry, I'm sorry. But it is my dream.

LISA: *(Looks down at herself.)* So how come I'm wearing this Mother Hubbard dress. I look like my mother. Don't I? Don't I look like somebody's mother, Ellie?

ELLIE: Yeah. You look like my mother.

GARY: I guess that's the way I see you, Lisa. You're sweet and ... er ... motherly.

LISA: Motherly?! Gary, wake up! I know I'm quiet and sweet

and no bimbo, but you see me as a mother, as motherly?

GARY: *(Confused, questioning)* I guess I just think you'd make a wonderful mother.

ELLIE: Oh, I get it. And I'd make a fun date, the good time girl — the dumb bimbo! I ought to ... to pinch you and wake you up!

GARY: This is getting us nowhere.

LISA: It's getting you nowhere. I should be home in bed fast asleep dreaming about Godunov or Baryshnikov — certainly not you, Gary.

GARY: I need you guys here to help me decide. Please. I'm so confused. I love you both. I know I can't marry you both.

ELLIE and LISA: Marry?

GARY: Yes. I want to marry one of you.

LISA: You do?

ELLIE: He does?

GARY: Yes! Of course! I do!

ELLIE: But who?

LISA: Me or the bimbo?

ELLIE: Lisa!

LISA: Ellie, that was Gary who thought that. Not me. Remember, this is his dream. Not mine.

ELLIE: Gary! Please! I'm not a bimbo! I'm a good girl, I just look like a bimbo. And I think that that is mostly your fault. You and that subconscious of yours. I think it needs a little redecorating.

GARY: But that's how I see you, Ellie.

ELLIE: Really? You think I look like *this?*

LISA: No! You don't look like that! Gary is making you look like that.

ELLIE: *(Really annoyed)* Oh, yeah. Right. I'm a figment of his sordid imagination. Stop that, Gary! OK?

GARY: I've tried, I've tried.

LISA: So who are you going to marry?

ELLIE: Yeah. Her or me? *(Just then TINA enters.)*

— 93 —

TINA: He's going to marry me!

ELLIE and LISA: *(Pointing to TINA)* Who the devil is she?!

GARY: *(Trying to hide TINA)* Er ... er ...

LISA: Been dreaming again, Gary?

ELLIE: She's probably just one of his dumb fantasies. Young guys like him have a lot of them, I hear.

LISA: Boys!

ELLIE: Dreamers! Is that all you boys do? *(Pointing to TINA)* Dream of fantasies like her?

GARY: Er ... well ...

LISA: That is all you do! And she is just another dumb fantasy.

TINA: *(Trying to peek out from behind GARY)* No, I'm not! I'm Gary's true love.

GARY: No, no! She's just a ... a ...

ELLIE and LISA: A *what?!*

GARY: Probably something I ate!

TINA, ELLIE and LISA: What?!

GARY: Yeah, yeah. She's probably just a result of those eight mini-burgers with onions I had last night after my baseball game. We won. You know? So me and the guys all went out to celebrate.

TINA, ELLIE and LISA: What are you saying, Gary?

GARY: She's just too many burgers or too many onions!

TINA, ELLIE and LISA: Oh, yeah?

TINA: *(Trying to peek out from behind GARY as he struggles to keep her hidden)* Wrong! I'm his dream girl! The one he really wants to marry!

GARY: Huh?

LISA: Well, then ... then ... you can just go ... go and marry that silly fantasy of yours. Because I don't love you any more! *(She begins to exit Stage Left.)*

GARY: Wait! Lisa, don't go! I love you!

TINA: *(Trying to peek out)* He says that to all the girls!

ELLIE: I'll bet! You're a no good, two-timing jerk, Gary! I've had it! I'm going home to bed! Good-by! I hope you and

your little fantasy are very happy together!

TINA: We will be!

GARY: *(To TINA)* Shut up!

TINA: Don't yell at me. This is your dream. Not mine.

ELLIE: Right! He has the most sordid subconscious of anyone I know. Good-by, jerk! *(She begins to exit Stage Right.)*

GARY: Ellie! Lisa! Wait! Don't go!

LISA: We're not going.

ELLIE: You're making us go.

LISA: This is your dream, not ours.

GARY: This is a nightmare!

ELLIE and LISA: You got that right. *(LISA and ELLIE exit, at opposite sides of stage.)*

GARY: Don't go!

TINA: Too late. They're gone.

GARY: Great. Just great. Now I have no one.

TINA: *(Snuggling closer to him)* You still have me, Gar.

GARY: Yeah. You. No doubt a bad case of indigestion.

TINA: *(Poses for him.)* Now do I look like a bad case of indigestion to you?

GARY: *(Looks at her very interested, then)* You're just something I ate. Onions.

TINA: Thanks a lot. But you're wrong.

GARY: I'm wrong? Great. OK. So who are you anyway? And how did you get into my dream? Do I know you?

TINA: I'm Tina. Remember?

GARY: *(Scratching his head)* Tina?

TINA: Yes. You know. Tina from the bus stop.

GARY: Tina from the bus stop? What bus stop?

TINA: You were waiting for the bus the other day.

GARY: What bus?

TINA: The one to the baseball game. And there I was. You couldn't take your eyes off me. I've been in your subconscious ever since. Way, way, way down in there —

deep down in there — with the dust and the fuzz balls of your relatively exciting past. Gary, you know, you have some pretty interesting thoughts hidden away down there?

GARY: Thanks. But I just lost Lisa and Ellie.

TINA: *(Dances around him.)* Well . . . maybe you don't really want them. Maybe you really want me. Besides, I'm the one who loves baseball.

GARY: Great. And I'll probably never see you again, either.

TINA: Sure you will. Just try that bus stop some day. Hey, maybe we can see a baseball game together.

GARY: Really?

TINA: Sure.

GARY: Great. I love baseball. But Lisa and Ellie don't.

TINA: Well, I do.

GARY: Terrific. Great. Hey, I'll check out that bus stop tomorrow. Will you be there?

TINA: You never know. I just might be there. After all, Gary, it is very true what all those romantics say: you really just never know when or where the right girl is going to come along. The one you'll end up marrying.

GARY: I guess so. *(Yawns)* Boy, suddenly I'm very tired.

TINA: You've had a very restless night. Right now you're actually home in bed tossing and turning in a sweat all tangled up in your bed sheets.

GARY: *(Goes and lies in bed.)* Yeah, right. *(He tosses and turns.)* I am restless . . . *(Yawns)* and so tired. *(He drifts off to sleep.)*

TINA: *(To audience)* I'd better get out of Gary's dream before he starts dreaming about monsters. I do hate monsters. *(Giggles, puts on a baseball cap she has hidden on her, and winks at audience.)* Night all. *(TINA exits as GARY snores, tosses and turns, as curtain falls.)*

The Car of the Future

PRODUCTION NOTES

PLAYERS: 2 women; 3 men; male and female extras as needed.

PLAYING TIME: 10 minutes.

COSTUMES: SUPER DAN in loud suit, MOLLY in gown, BILL and AMY and TRADE SHOW GOERS in casual clothes, MAN IN WHITE and others in white uniform.

PROPERTIES: Microphone, big red key, plastic soda bottle.

SOUND EFFECTS: SUPER DAN talks into a microphone that makes his voice echo as if he is in big auditorium. Loud ticking.

The Car of the Future

CHARACTERS: SUPER DAN, car salesman; MOLLY, model; BILL, car buyer; AMY, Bill's girl friend; MAN IN WHITE, an asylum doctor; EXTRAS, for Men and Women in white and Trade Show Goers, Extras as needed.

TIME: Today.

SETTING: Car show.

AT RISE: Four chairs to represent a car of the future. MOLLY acts like a model, pointing to car's features as SUPER DAN talks on microphone about them. TRADE SHOW GOERS pass by.

SUPER DAN: **Ladies and gentlemen, children of all ages, witness the car of the future — the Laser Beam Mark Five. Look at its sleek lines, its luxurious interior. Can you afford to drive anything else?** *(BILL and AMY stop to look at car.)* **Hi, Super Dan's the name, cars of the future's the game. And what are your names?**

BILL: **I'm Bill and this is my girl friend, Amy.**

SUPER DAN: *(Shaking their hands till they hurt)* **Howdy, howdy. Glad to meet ya. Looking for a new car, are you?**

BILL: **Well, not exactly.**

AMY: **We were just looking.**

BILL: *(Trying to walk away)* **Yes, just looking.** *(He tries to walk away, but SUPER DAN grabs him and pulls him back.)*

SUPER DAN: **So look!**

AMY and BILL: *(Nervous)* **We're looking. We're looking.**

SUPER DAN: **Just looking? Just looking!**

AMY: **Yes!**

BILL: **Yes!**

SUPER DAN: **No, no, no! This is your time to buy. This is your car. The Laser Beam Mark Five is for you, a young couple on the move.** *(MOLLY nods and smiles and points to everything SUPER DAN points to.)*

AMY: It looks like four chairs. *(MOLLY frowns.)*

SUPER DAN: Shush! *(Points to audience.)* **They think it's a car of the future.** *(MOLLY nods and points to chairs.)* **See? Even our model Molly agrees. Yes! Look at those sleek lines, that luxurious interior.**

BILL: *(Looking at MOLLY)* **She is pretty.**

AMY: *(Angry)* **Bill!**

SUPER DAN: **Not Molly!** *(MOLLY and SUPER DAN point to chairs.)* **The car! Corinthian leather, genuine mahogany, eye-dazzling chrome and unbreakable, real plastic!**

BILL: **Real plastic?**

SUPER DAN: **Unbreakable, space-age plastic. Used to make rocket nose cones.**

AMY: **Rocket nose cones?**

SUPER DAN: **Yep. Guaranteed not to melt down unless the temperature goes above twelve thousand degrees centigrade!**

BILL: **Really?**

SUPER DAN: **Would I lie to you?** *(MOLLY nods yes, then quickly shakes her head no when SUPER DAN looks at her.)*

BILL: **Look, no offense, but we were looking for something more . . . more . . .**

AMY: **Car like.**

BILL: **Right. With four-wheel drive.**

SUPER DAN: **This is better! It has five-wheel drive.**

BILL: **What?**

SUPER DAN: **You heard me. This baby climbs mountains in the snow, sleet or rain.** *(Goes to open hood, mimes that.)* **And look at this engine.**

BILL: *(Not knowing what else to say, looks)* **Er, great. How many miles to the gallon does it get?**

SUPER DAN: **City or freeway?**

AMY: **Both.**

SUPER DAN: **About a million in the city, maybe two or three million on the freeway.**

BILL: I don't believe it.

AMY: Neither do I. No car gets that many miles on a gallon of gas.

SUPER DAN: Gas? Who said it uses gas?

BILL: It doesn't run on gas? So it gets that on diesel fuel?

SUPER DAN: Nope.

AMY: Is it one of those new solar-powered cars?

SUPER DAN: No, young lady. Not quite.

BILL: Then what does it run on?

SUPER DAN: Plutonium.

AMY and BILL: *(Shocked, backing away)* **Plutonium?!**

SUPER DAN: Finest grade you can get from used nuclear reactors. We finally found a safe — well, almost safe — use for the stuff. There is still one problem.

BILL: Just one problem?

SUPER DAN: Yes. You have to be very careful in traffic.

AMY: I'll bet.

SUPER DAN: Yes. One fender bender and there goes the neighborhood — actually, the city.

BILL: *(Backing away a bit more)* **Are these cars very popular?**

SUPER DAN: Not with the insurance companies — or the gas station owners.

AMY: I wonder why.

SUPER DAN: Well, the plutonium tends to force the insurance companies to raise their rates. And then there's a very big deductible.

BILL: A thousand dollars?

SUPER DAN: A billion.

AMY: A billion?

SUPER DAN: Hey, when someone clips your fender and you end up blowing up a city, people are likely to sue.

BILL: I'm not sure if I can afford the rates.

AMY: Right. And they're usually higher for younger drivers, you know.

SUPER DAN: *(Slaps AMY on back.)* **Don't worry! We can work** something out. You have a rich father, young lady?

AMY: No.

SUPER DAN: *(Pointing to BILL)* Does he?

BILL: No.

SUPER DAN: A rich uncle?

AMY: Look, Super Dan. We're only high school seniors. I sell hamburgers.

BILL: And I pump gas after school.

SUPER DAN: Gas? A dying business! With these new plutonium engines, gas is going to be useless in months. Take my word for it, get into plutonium. *(MOLLY nods.)*

AMY: Isn't plutonium bad for you?

BILL: Right. It's the world's most deadly poison.

SUPER DAN: Nonsense!

AMY: You're saying Bill is wrong?

SUPER DAN: I'm just saying plutonium is no more dangerous than ... than ... er ...

BILL: Than what?

SUPER DAN: I can't think of anything at the moment, but I'll tell you this much: plutonium is perfectly safe so long as you don't eat it, breathe it, or jar it too violently.

AMY: As in fender benders.

SUPER DAN: Exactly. So what do you think? A thousand down and a thousand a week? I can give you ten years to pay? And there's only twenty-eight per cent financing.

BILL: Twenty-eight per cent? I thought it was supposed to be two-point-eight per cent.

AMY: That's what I heard on TV.

SUPER DAN: That's on those old gas guzzlers. The plutonium jobs have slightly high risks. Some drivers sort of ... er ... default on their loans.

BILL: What do they do? — *(MOLLY holds her ears.)*

AMY and BILL: *(Almost laughing)* Explode?

SUPER DAN: Right! How did you guess? Ever wonder where the Grand Canyon came from? It used to be an eight-lane freeway. Then the Laser Beam Mark Five came along. *(MOLLY nods.)* So what do you think? You want to put her on a lay-away plan for Christmas?

BILL: I don't think so.

SUPER DAN: She'd be a great stocking stuffer. *(To AMY)* Wouldn't you want to wake up Christmas morning and find this beauty in your stocking.

AMY: Not really. I prefer my foot in my stocking.

SUPER DAN: Did I show you these great tires? *(SUPER DAN kicks a chair.)* Now that's a tire. You want to know about a great set of wheels? This is a great set of wheels. All five of them. Great, eh? Want to know more?

BILL: Not really.

SUPER DAN: Well I'm going to tell you anyway. These are totally synthetic. Know what they're made of?

AMY: I'm almost afraid to ask.

SUPER DAN: Well, I'm not afraid to tell you. These are made of old soda bottles.

BILL: What?

AMY: Come on. Soda bottles? Yeah, sure.

SUPER DAN: I'm telling you, these tires used to be soda bottles. You know, those plastic ones. *(MOLLY holds one up.)* We recycled them. And get this. You get a flat, know what you do?

BILL: Take it back and get a nickel deposit?

SUPER DAN: *(Amazed)* Yeah! How did you guess?

AMY: It was easy.

SUPER DAN: Most people think I'm nuts *(MOLLY makes a crazy sign with her finger twirling beside her temple)*, but not you. Anyhow, where were we?

BILL: Spinning our wheels.

SUPER DAN: Yes, yes. Tires. These never wear out. They do have one slight problem.

AMY: And what's that?

SUPER DAN: They don't come with a spare. So if you get a flat, you're in trouble.

BILL: But I thought you said they never wear out.

SUPER DAN: They don't, but they do get flats. Know why?

AMY: Nails in the road?

SUPER DAN: No, no. People forget to put the bottle cap back on after inflating them. And look at that radio.

BILL: Stereo?

SUPER DAN: Intergalactic.

AMY: Intergalactic? What do you get on it? UFO's?

SUPER DAN: Yep. Talk about far out sound, eh? You got it in this baby.

BILL: I don't believe this. Whoever heard of a car with a plutonium engine, old soda bottle tires and an intergalactic radio?

AMY: Not me.

SUPER DAN: You must have. I just told you about it. *(MOLLY nods.)*

BILL: Yeah, right. But you're nuts!

AMY: Right. You're crazy.

SUPER DAN: Oh, sure. I'm a raving maniac. Mad! A loony! Bonkers!

AMY and BILL: *(Backing away a bit)* No offense.

SUPER DAN: Sure, sure. I bet you say that to all the car salesmen.

BILL: No. Only to those who try to sell us plutonium cars.

SUPER DAN: I'm telling you, it's the latest thing! What, you prefer one of those old gas guzzlers? Or one of those silly solar-powered jalopies?

AMY: We just want a little jeep.

BILL: One with four-wheel drive.

SUPER DAN: Junk! Bombs!

BILL: And a plutonium car is not a bomb?

SUPER DAN: Well, just a little one.

AMY: *(Backing away more, and hiding behind BILL)* How ... how little?

SUPER DAN: Ten . . . maybe twenty megatons.

AMY and BILL: What?!

SUPER DAN: *(Pulls out a big red key.)* **Relax! She's not armed.**

AMY and BILL: *(Scared)* **Not armed?!**

SUPER DAN: **Nope. To arm her,** *(Hands key to MOLLY)*, **you have to put this key in the ignition** *(MOLLY does)*, **turn it** *(MOLLY does)*, **and wait for the ticking.**

AMY and BILL: **Ticking?!**

SUPER DAN: *(We hear ticking.)* **Yes, ticking. There it is. Now she's armed.**

BILL: **How long do we have to go?**

SUPER DAN: *(MOLLY counts down with her fingers as SUPER DAN counts down.)* **Ten . . . nine . . . eight . . . seven . . .** *(AMY and BILL hug each other in fear)* **six . . . five . . . four . . . three . . . two . . . one . . . zero!**

AMY and BILL: *(Holding their ears)* **Oh, no!** *(Just then MEN and WOMEN in white coats enter.)*

MAN IN WHITE: **There he is! Grab him!** *(SUPER DAN tries to escape.)* **Stop him!** *(MEN and WOMEN in white coats grab SUPER DAN.)* **Got you! Take him away!**

BILL: *(To MAN in white)* **You mean this is not the Laser Beam Mark Five?** *(Pointing to chairs)*

MAN IN WHITE: **The what?**

AMY: **A car of the future. With a plutonium engine.**

MAN IN WHITE: **What are you? Nuts?**

BILL: **But Super Dan said** *(Points to chairs)* **this was the car of the future!**

AMY: **Right. Super Dan told us.**

MAN IN WHITE: **Super Dan? Him? Look, last week he thought he was Henry Ford, the week before that he thought he was Lee Iacocca.**

BILL: **What is he? Nuts?**

MAN IN WHITE: **How would you feel if your head was run over by a double stretch limo lemon you sold a little old lady from Pasadena?** *(Curtain)*

Slob School

PRODUCTION NOTES

PLAYERS: 2 females, 1 male.

PLAYING TIME: About 12 minutes.

COSTUMES: AMANDA in very fashionable business suit, very proper. CHARLES in tux. RHONDA in greasy coveralls and boots.

PROPERTIES: White silk napkins, spoons, forks, bowls of soup, jacket.

SOUND EFFECTS: Knocking and banging at door from off stage, doorbell.

Slob School

CHARACTERS: AMANDA WHINTHROPE, teaches manners and etiquette; CHARLES HATHAWAY, her new assistant and "former" slob; RHONDA, an ill-mannered slob.

TIME: Today.

SETTING: Combination school room/dining room with neatly set table for three, Center Stage.

AT RISE: AMANDA and CHARLES enter.

CHARLES: So you really believe that there is no such thing as a true, genetically predetermined slob, Ms. Whinthrope? Born slobs, so to speak?

AMANDA: Yes, that is correct, Charles. Slobs are not born. They are made.

CHARLES: You mean they get it from their parents?

AMANDA: You can't just fault the parents, Charles. It's the whole environment. Society in general. Manners, etiquette, it's all gone to pot! And I, Amanda Whinthrope, owner and operator of the Amanda Whinthrope School of Manners and Social Graces for the Hopelessly Slobby, firmly believe that one can just as easily be taught to be a well-mannered, bon vivant as he or she can so easily degenerate into a socially unacceptable slob.

CHARLES: I hope you're right.

AMANDA: Charles, if you don't believe I can change a slob into a prince or princess, what do you think I turned you into and why do you choose to work here?

CHARLES: Well, the grease monkey job down at Sloppy Joe's Luborama was taken. So, heck, I said, I'll give slob school a shot, and here I am.

AMANDA: I hate when people call my establishment slob school! It's so uncouth!

CHARLES: When I was a slob, that's what I called this place.

AMANDA: Yes, but fortunately, you've changed.

CHARLES: You really think so?

AMANDA: Oh, yes. Just look at you. *(She does.)* There you are, a former oily, grease-stained slob completely transformed into the epitome of style and grace.

CHARLES: *(Itchy, and uncomfortable in his tux)* Yeah, that's me. A real gent.

AMANDA: Gentleman, Charles. Not gent. Gent is what they put on restroom doors in gas stations. You are a gentleman, one I created out of mud and grease. So how do you like being a gentleman, Charles?

CHARLES: I don't know, Ms. Whinthrope.

AMANDA: Please, Charles, call me Amanda — but only when we're alone.

CHARLES: Sure, Ms. Whin — I mean, sure, Amanda. And you can call me Chuck.

AMANDA: *(Curtsying to him)* Thank you, Chuck.

CHARLES: *(Bowing to her)* You're welcome, Amanda.

AMANDA: *(Straightening up table setting)* So, Chuck, how do you like being a gentleman?

CHARLES: Well, I'll tell ya, it feels sort of weird. I'm not used to eating with clean hands and wearing this here monkey suit.

AMANDA: Tuxedo, Chuck. It's a tux.

CHARLES: Right. *(Itchy and uncomfortable)* Tux. It makes me feel sort of itchy. I still wish you would have let me wear my coveralls.

AMANDA: Good lord, no! This is a school of style, etiquette, and manners — not a Luborama! You must wear that tux at all times and remember all the manners I taught you. Will you do that, Chuck?

CHARLES: I'll give it my best shot, Mandy.

AMANDA: That's Amanda, Chuck. Let's not get too personal. Remember, this is merely a business relationship.

CHARLES: Right. Business. Like me and Sloppy Joe last

year down at the Luborama.

AMANDA: I do hope not. Now, you remember how I taught you how to eat?

CHARLES: Yes.

AMANDA: Then let's sit at the table and practice. *(CHARLES sits as AMANDA paces about.)* Are you comfortable?

CHARLES: *(Squirming and slouching)* Yeah, sort of.

AMANDA: Good, then stop squirming and sit up straight! *(CHARLES does.)* Excellent. Now, remember what I told you to never ever do when eating?

CHARLES: Er . . . Oh, yeah. Never ever use my hands to eat. Use my spoon and fork at all times, especially when eating soup.

AMANDA: Good. Correct. But what else, Chuck?

CHARLES: Errr. Let's see . . . *(Thinks, picks up napkin.)* Don't blow my nose in my napkin?

AMANDA: That's not what I was thinking of, but still I absolutely forbid you to ever do that! These are my best silk napkins!

CHARLES: No nose blowing! *(As AMANDA paces like a drill sergeant)* OK, so that wasn't it. So what else is there?

AMANDA: I'll give you a hint.

CHARLES: Great. I love hints.

AMANDA: Good. When eating soup, what don't we ever do?

CHARLES: *(Thinks, scratches his head.)* Ummm — make jokes about flies doing the backstroke in it?

AMANDA: No! No! Think!

CHARLES: *(Squeezes his eyes shut and strains to think.)* Ummm, we . . . we . . . er — *(Opens his eyes and points at her.)* Oh, I know!

AMANDA: What?!

CHARLES: We never slurp it!

AMANDA: Right! We never ever slurp our soup! Only uncouth slobs slurp their soup. Well-mannered persons *(Waiting for CHARLES to answer)* simply . . . simply, Chuck, what do well-mannered persons do when eating soup?!

CHARLES: Stick the spoon in their mouth, shut their mouth, pull out the spoon and ... and ...

AMANDA: *(Slaps him on the back.)* **Swallow!**

CHARLES: *(Choking, then)* **R-right!** *(Trying to catch his breath)*

AMANDA: Yes. Breathe, Chuck.

CHARLES: Right. Breathe. *(He catches his breath.)* **Breathe.**

AMANDA: Yes. Now you see? I told you I could transform you into a gentleman.

CHARLES: It's amazing, Amanda. Do you think all the girls will like me now?

AMANDA: Did they like you before, Chuck?

CHARLES: No. They said I was an oily slime.

AMANDA: It must have been all that grease and oil from the Luborama they were referring to.

CHARLES: I don't know.

AMANDA: *(Thinks about it. Checks her watch.)* **Up, Chuck!**

CHARLES: *(Shocked at the pun)* **Now?! At the table?**

AMANDA: Yes.

CHARLES: You sure?

AMANDA: Yes! Now! Up, Chuck!

CHARLES: OK, but I didn't think it was polite to do that at dinner table. But if you insist.

AMANDA: I insist! Up, Chuck!

CHARLES: You got it, but I'd stand back if I were you. *(He starts to stick his finger in his mouth and to gag.)*

AMANDA: *(Horrified)* **What are you doing?!**

CHARLES: You told me to up chuck.

AMANDA *(Pulls him up)* I meant for you to get up, Charles!

CHARLES: *(He jumps up.)* **Ohhh!** *(Doorbell)*

AMANDA: Our first student. *(Hops around.)* **I'm so excited.**

CHARLES: Is hopping proper etiquette?

AMANDA: *(Quickly controls herself)* **Who's hopping? I was just a bit excited.** *(Banging at door)*

CHARLES: Sounds like they are, too. I just hope you're as

lucky with them as you were with me. *(Looking proud)* I've changed.

AMANDA: Yes, yes. I'm sure. *(Even louder knocking, then to wing)* Enter! *(RHONDA enters; even CHARLES is horrified at her sloppiness.)*

CHARLES: *(Whispers to AMANDA.)* Good luck, teach.

RHONDA: *(To AMANDA and CHARLES)* Howdy. *(To AMANDA)* My name's Rhonda Plopper. You the one that's gonna turn me into a lady or what?

AMANDA: Er ... yes.

RHONDA: Good, 'cause the guys don't like me like this. They say I make them sick.

CHARLES: Really?

RHONDA: Yep. They wanna throw up when they see me.

AMANDA: Really?

RHONDA: Yep. *(To AMANDA)* Who's this wimp? The local undertaker?

CHARLES: I'm a gentleman.

RHONDA: Could have fooled me, bub. So who is he?

AMANDA: *(Still a bit in shock)* Er ... he ... he's my ... er ... my —

CHARLES: *(Whispering to AMANDA)* Assistant.

AMANDA: My assistant.

RHONDA: Oh, yeah? Funny. He looks like an undertaker. So ... where do we start? I want to get started here so I can get a guy to like me before they all get too old. *(Nudging CHARLES with her elbow)* Know what I mean?

CHARLES: Errr.

RHONDA: So where do we start? Eatin', drinkin', clothes? My duds OK, or am I a little out of fashion?

AMANDA: *(Looking at RHONDA)* Yes. A bit out of fashion.

CHARLES: A bit?!

AMANDA: Etiquette, Charles. Remember our etiquette.

RHONDA: Yeah, bub. You could have hurt a lady's feelings, you know.

CHARLES: Lady? What lady?

RHONDA: I was referring to me. My feelings.

AMANDA: Yes. Now, Rhonda, let's begin by learning the proper way to eat soup.

CHARLES: I'm real good at that.

RHONDA: I know how to do that. *(RHONDA turns chair backwards, straddles it up to table, picks up bowl of soup and gets ready to drink it.)* **First you blow on the stuff, and then you drink the stuff.** *(She does, slurping loudly.)*

CHARLES: Oh, boy. She's slurping. She's a slob.

RHONDA: Really?

AMANDA: I'm afraid so, but don't you worry. We'll transform you.

CHARLES: Anything's possible.

AMANDA: Charles, will you demonstrate the proper way to sit at the dining room table and the correct method for eating hot soup?

CHARLES: Certainly, Ms. Whinthrope. *(He sits at table and picks up spoon.)* **Like so.** *(Demonstrates eating soup.)* **One never slurps! It's rude. Correct, Ms. Whinthrope?**

AMANDA: Exactly, Charles. Very good. Now, Rhonda, do you think you can do that?

RHONDA: *(Watching CHARLES)* **Well ... I don't know. It looks kinda complicated. Let's see.** *(She gets up and tries to set the chair correctly and can't seem to get it just right. She tries moving it a few times, then is satisfied that it's correctly placed, she sits and picks up spoon, holds it exactly like CHARLES is holding his and eats exactly like CHARLES.)* **How's that? Am I doing it right?**

AMANDA: Yes! I think she's got it! Perfect! *(As CHARLES and RHONDA eat)* **Wonderful, that's it! Slowly, don't rush. Don't slurp, no gobbling, easy. Excellent!**

RHONDA: Hey, I think I got it! Am I doing OK at eating soup or what?

AMANDA: You're doing just fine. But we mustn't talk while we eat.

RHONDA: Oh, yeah. Right. But you know, I was a little confused there for a while, you know, when we first started eating. But once you get the hang of it, and you get the rhythm just right, it's sort of easy.

CHARLES: Soup's not bad either. *(To AMANDA)* What is it?

AMANDA: *(As CHARLES and RHONDA eat)* You like it?

CHARLES and RHONDA: Yeah.

AMANDA: It's frogs' leg bisque. *(CHARLES and RHONDA spray the soup out of their mouths toward audience and begin to gag and choke as AMANDA slaps them on the back.)* Are you OK? Are you all right?

CHARLES and RHONDA: *Frogs' leg bisque?!*

AMANDA: Yes. Was it too hot?

RHONDA: It was too froggie! Yuk!

CHARLES: I hate frogs!

AMANDA: Oh, you see, that is a problem.

CHARLES: Why?

AMANDA: Not liking frogs' leg soup is totally uncultured.

RHONDA: It is?

AMANDA: Oh, yes. If you are to be cultured, well-mannered, you are going to have to get used to eating all varieties of things.

CHARLES: Like what?

AMANDA: Like frogs' legs, fish eggs, and even birds' nest soup.

RHONDA: *(Standing, shaking her head and waving her hands)* Uh-uh, not me. I'm a meat and potatoes person. I don't eat no dead frogs or birds' nests! No way.

AMANDA: But what about the boys? They like a girl who likes fish eggs and frogs' legs.

CHARLES: *(Getting up)* I don't.

RHONDA: You don't?

CHARLES: No way. Not me. I'm a meat and potatoes guy.

RHONDA: You are?

CHARLES: Heck, yeah. And chili dogs, tacos, pizza!

RHONDA: Me too! Hey, Chuck, you're all right for an undertaker. *(Slaps him on the back, nearly knocking him over.)*

CHARLES: *(Regaining his balance)* Thanks, Rhonda. But I'm not really an undertaker.

AMANDA: Right! He a gentleman!

RHONDA: *(To CHARLES)* You are?

CHARLES: Actually, last year I used to work at Sloppy Joe's Luborama, but they aren't hiring this year.

RHONDA: I know! I wanted to work there too. I love grease and dirt and grime and oil.

CHARLES: So do I!

RHONDA: No!

CHARLES: Yeah! I wallow in it!

AMANDA: Until I turned him into a gentleman! Right, Charles? Right?!

CHARLES: *(Taking off tux jacket and putting on his sloppy jacket which was on floor under table)* I'm sorry, Amanda, but I quit. I'm going back to working in the muck of life.

RHONDA: Me, too. I hate being a lady.

CHARLES: But you are a lady, Rhonda!

RHONDA and AMANDA: *Really?*

RHONDA: I am?

CHARLES: *(Wipes grease off her face with napkin.)* Sure you are. Under all that dirt and grime is a real lady. A very pretty one, too. I knew it all the time.

RHONDA: *(As AMANDA cries over filthy napkin)* And I knew you were a great guy, too, Charles.

CHARLES: Call me Chuck.

RHONDA: OK, Chuck. *(They don't know what to say.)*

CHARLES and RHONDA: So . . . what do we do now?

AMANDA: The proper etiquette is to ask someone out!

CHARLES: Right!

RHONDA: So . . . Chuck, you want to go out for a chili dog or something?

CHARLES: Sure. Then if you want, we can go watch them

change the oil down at Sloppy Joe's Luborama.

RHONDA: *(Hugs CHARLES.)* **What a guy! You're great, Chuck!**

AMANDA: **What about manners, charm, style, etiquette?**

RHONDA and CHARLES: *(Taking two napkins)* **We'll clean our hands before the chili dogs.**

RHONDA: **And maybe even after.**

CHARLES: **Right. Maybe!** *(CHARLES and RHONDA leave happily hand-in-hand. As curtain falls, AMANDA sits in chair as RHONDA first did. AMANDA slurps soup loudly.)*

Dear Hattie

PRODUCTION NOTES

PLAYERS: 3 women, 2 men, 1 either male or female.

PLAYING TIME: About 15 minutes.

COSTUMES: MAILMAN in uniform, ARTIE in suit, MS. JOHNSON in business suit, all others in casual clothes.

PROPERTIES: Portable typewriter, typing paper, old files, paper, mailbag, letters, handkerchief.

LIGHTING EFFECTS: Spotlight comes up on players and fades as noted in script.

Dear Hattie

CHARACTERS: ARTIE PETERS, has just become the new advice-to-lovelorn columnist Dear Hattie; MAILMAN, can be man or woman; CONFUSED IN CANARSIE; ALONE IN ALBUQUERQUE; MS. JOHNSON, newspaper publisher and ARTIE's boss; TERRY, ARTIE's girl friend and also "Heartbroken in Hoboken."

TIME: Today.

SETTING: Stage Left is Dear Hattie's office. There is a desk with large piles of letters. A small portable typewriter is in center of desk. Chair behind desk so ARTIE faces audience when sitting. Trash can to side of desk. Filing cabinets to left and right of large portrait of older woman that hangs on wall. Beneath it are the words DEAR HATTIE. Portrait is surrounded with black crepe. Stage Right is a stool where letter writers sit and read answers to their letters.

AT RISE: MAILMAN enters with big mailbag of letters for "Dear Hattie."

MAILMAN: *(Hefting the big bag of mail onto ARTIE's desk)* **This is for Dear Hattie. Where is she? I think she's great. And such a nice lady. You know what I mean?**

ARTIE: Sorry, but she isn't here.

MAILMAN: *(Looking around)* **So where is she?**

ARTIE: You're looking at her — I mean, him. I'm her — or him.

MAILMAN: But you're not Hattie. You're a guy. I'm confused.

ARTIE: *You're* **confused? What about** *me* **?**

MAILMAN: But I thought the Dear Hattie's advice-to-the-lovelorn column was written by a woman.

ARTIE: It was until the real Dear Hattie went bonkers and jumped in front of an extremely large wedding party.

MAILMAN: What happened to her?

ARTIE: They say all these letters *(Pulls dozens of them out the bag)* drove her nuts. Too much stress, I guess. She couldn't take all the heartbreaking stories in these letters.

MAILMAN: So the real Dear Hattie is . . . dead.

ARTIE: As a doornail.

MAILMAN: Gosh. How'd she die?

ARTIE: They tell me it happened at one of the weddings she suggested in a letter. First, she was bombarded with tons of rice, and then she was run over by forty-two white wedding limos with "Just Married" signs hung on them. They say she died happy. *(Getting nervous and angry)* But if you ask me, this job drove her nuts! Even her husband couldn't take it! And he was a stress counselor!

MAILMAN: Hey, relax, buddy.

ARTIE: The name's Artie!

MAILMAN: OK, Artie. But you have to learn to take it easy, roll with the punches.

ARTIE: That's what Ms. Johnson, my boss, said.

MAILMAN: She's right. So do you think you can handle this job *(Dumps out bag of letters)* and all these letters?

ARTIE: *(Nervous)* I don't know. I really don't know. I've only been on this job a week and already I'm going crazy — and my own love life isn't getting any better.

MAILMAN: Your girl friend doesn't like you doing this, making believe you're a woman *(Laughs)*, **Dear Hattie?**

ARTIE: Shush! No one knows I'm *(Points to portrait)* her, not even my girl friend!

MAILMAN: So why is she mad at you?

ARTIE: She thinks I'm going out with other women. It must be all these letters. *(Tosses some in trash can.)* The other night I called her Sweetlips from Seattle.

MAILMAN: And she doesn't live in Seattle?

ARTIE: No. She lives in Hoboken, New Jersey.

MAILMAN: Oh, boy. And now she thinks you're dating other women, but you're really not?

ARTIE: *(Trying to hide the fact he is dating other woman)* **Well . . . that's not the point! But if you ask me, I think she's so mad at me, she's starting to date other guys! I'm so confused. What do you think I should do?**

MAILMAN: **Hey, wait a second. I'm just a mailman. You're Dear Hattie. You figure it out.**

ARTIE: **All I know is I am really mad at everyone, especially all these** *(Tosses some letters in trash can)* **crybabies! I hate them! I hate them! All of them!**

MAILMAN: *(Backs away)* **Take it easy, buddy.**

ARTIE: **The name's Artie! Not buddy! I'm Artie! Not Dear Hattie! I'm Artie! Artie! You understand?!**

MAILMAN: **OK, OK, Artie. Sit down. Relax. Try some meditation or deep breathing. You don't want to blow a gasket or something.**

ARTIE: *(Sits down and tries to relax, draws a few deep breaths.)* **I am not going to go bonkers, I am not going to go bonkers, I am not going to go bonkers.**

MAILMAN: **That's the ticket. I have two more bags of mail for you at the post office. I'll bring them up later. Have a nice day.**

ARTIE: *(Obviously more annoyed, but trying to maintain control, faster)* **I am not going to go bonkers, I am not going to go bonkers, I am not going to go bonkers.**

MAILMAN: *(Scared, quickly exits.)* **That's the ticket. Remain calm. Take deep breaths. Relax.**

ARTIE: **Easy for a mailman to say.** *(Tosses letters about.)* **They just have to deliver all these letters! I have to answer them.** *(Looks through letters, finds one.)* **Look at this wimp.** *(Reads letter very sarcastically, faking crying.)* **Dear Hattie, my girl friend and I have been dating for nearly a year now. She keeps asking me when I'm going to marry her. What do you think I should do? I know she loves me, well, I think she does. Should I tell her I want to graduate first or what? Please help! Signed, Confused in Canarsie.**

(Angry, puts letter down and puts typing paper in typewriter and begins to answer letter as light fades out on him and spotlight comes up on CONFUSED IN CANARSIE.) **Dear Confused in Canarsie . . .**

CONFUSED IN CANARSIE: *(Reads answer.)* **If you ask me, Mr. Confused, you should dump that dumb girl friend of yours. Take it from me, all women are alike. No. I, Dear Hattie, am different. But these other women, all they want is just one thing from men — and we know what that is. Money! So take my advice: dump her! Dump them all! Signed, Yours Totally Unconfused, Dear Hattie.** *(Stands up and walks around really angry, or as angry as he can get.)* **Right! I'll dump her. So what if she's a sweet, kind, loving, beautiful, intelligent angel. Dear Hattie is right: all women are alike. I'll dump her and join the French Foreign Legion like my dad wants me to do. I'm through with women!** *(Storms off, really angry as light fades out on him and comes up on ARTIE.)*

ARTIE: *(Finishing typing)* **That should tell him!** *(Goes to filing cabinet and looks in it.)* **Look at these old files of Dear Hattie's.** *(Begins to throw files in trash.)* **Sweetness and light is all over with! Hattie's old answers to readers' questions are out of here. Your way is over, Dear Hattie. It's my turn now.** *(Laughs fiendishly.)* **I'm here to straighten some dingbats out.** *(Looks at some answers he's just taken from filing cabinet. They are copies of letters the real Dear Hattie wrote.)* **Look at this. Dear Hattie's answer to a girl called Unsure in Union who asked her what to do on a first date. Listen to this.** *(Reads letter very sarcastically in high mock female voice.)* **Dear Unsure, everyone is confused on a first date, especially today with all the passion being shown on TV and in the movies. A girl just doesn't know what to do. Should she be full of passion or should she be cool and a bit aloof on a first date or any date for that matter? If she's passionate, the boy might like it, but will he respect**

her, or will she respect herself? If she's cool and aloof, will the boy think she's a prude and dump her for a more passionate date? These are age-old questions. The only answer I can give you, my dear Unsure, is to be yourself. You can't put on an act in these situations. You have to trust your heart and your feelings and not let TV or the movies or anyone else turn you into a robot. You are you. You have to do what you feel is best for you as a person. After all, you are the one you have to live with. So just relax and try to be yourself on that first date. They are always the hardest. I remember. So be yourself and if the boy doesn't like what you are, don't worry, you'll find another — as long as you're true to you. *(Tears up letter.)* What baloney! Who would ever believe such drivel! *(Tosses more files into trash.)* This stuff is all old hat. Today life is not all hearts and flowers as it was for you, Dear Hattie. *(Looks at another letter.)* Speaking of hearts and flowers, listen to this. It's to some guy who calls himself Lonely from Louisville. *(Reads it sarcastically in high-pitched voice.)* Dear Lonely, we're all lonely sometimes. So don't feel just because you and your long-time girl friend broke up, you'll never find another girl to love. True. Breaking up is hard to do, but as Yogi Berra once said, "It ain't over till it's over." And it ain't over yet. You're a good person. You're young. You can't sit home feeling blue. Yes, I know you are hurting right now. That's normal. But if you want to feel better, you have to pick yourself up and get back into the stream of life and back into the dating scene. So call two girls you know today and call me in the morning. I want to meet a nice guy like you myself. There aren't too many men around these days who'll admit they too can be hurt and can be lonely. You are a rare man. Signed, With Deep Respect, Dear Hattie. *(Annoyed)* What claptrap! *(Tears letter up and tosses it into trash can, then throws rest of filed letters into trash. ARTIE slams filing cabinet closed and goes back to desk and reads another letter from mailbag.)* **Look at this girl. She calls herself Alone in Albuquerque.** *(Reads letter.)* **Dear Hattie, I feel so bad. I'm away at school and I miss my family and my friends from back at home. Especially Ralph, my basset hound. Oh, yes, I also kind of miss Lenny, my boy friend. To be perfectly honest, I'm not sure who I miss most. My parents, my dog, or Lenny. I think it's my dog. Hattie, I feel so guilty. I know I should miss my parents more than my dog and Lenny more than everyone. But I don't. Am I a rat or what? Please help me. I don't know who to talk to or who to write to anymore. When I'm home, I talk to Ralph a lot. Mom and Dad are usually out of town on business and Lenny is only interested in baseball and football. So at home I only have my dog Ralph to talk to. Here I have no one. I haven't made friends yet. I'm new here. Do you think I need help? Should I make friends? Should I speak to a counselor or just get a parakeet or maybe a goldfish? They don't allow dogs in the school dorm. Signed, Alone in Albuquerque.** *(ARTIE tosses the letter away.)* **What a crybaby! Does she need help? Yeah. And I'm just the guy to give it to her.** *(He puts paper in typewriter and starts typing as light fades out on him and comes up on ALONE IN ALBUQUERQUE.)*

ALONE IN ALBUQUERQUE: *(Reading letter)* **Dear Alone, if you ask me, you should stop sniveling, you crybaby! Too bad that you're all alone! You make me sick! You miss your mommy and daddy and that dumb dog Ralph? Too bad! And what a dumb name for a dog! And you have a boy friend? I'm amazed! I would think a crybaby like you would have a teddy bear or a security blankie. You ask me if you need help? The answer is *yes!* You should look up "wimp" and "baby" in the school library, because that's what you are! Signed, Totally Fed Up with You, Dear Hattie.** *(In tears, takes out handkerchief and blows her nose.)* **I thought I was a good person. No one loves me.**

Not even Dear Hattie. I have nothing to live for! Well, there is that school dance next weekend. I could make friends. But is it worth it? Maybe I should write Dear Hattie another letter. Oh, why does life seem so bleak at times? *(Blows her nose and exits as light fades out on her and comes up on ARTIE.)*

ARTIE: There. That ought to take care of her! *(MS. JOHNSON enters.)*

MS. JOHNSON: *(Angry)* Arthur Peters!

ARTIE: Oh, no! My boss, Ms. Johnson, our publisher! She warned me to be nice to our readers. *(Hides letters he just wrote.)* I better hide these letters I just wrote.

MS. JOHNSON: There you are, Peters! I want a few words with you.

ARTIE: Anything wrong, Ms. Johnson?

MS. JOHNSON: I've just come by to remind you of our high standards here at the paper. We feel we must honor the memory of our dear, departed Dear Hattie with decent, caring, and honest advice from her — in this case, you.

ARTIE: Oh, yes, yes. I understand. Honesty, decency and . . . er . . . and —

MS. JOHNSON: Caring!

ARTIE: Right. Caring.

MS. JOHNSON: Exactly. We are a caring newspaper and it's a wonderful person whose shoes you have to fill. So remember, never hurt anyone's feelings. If I so much as hear you've caused one person to shed a single tear, it's out you go. And we all know your relationship with your girl friend Terry whatshername is a bit rocky now, but I trust that that will not affect your answers to those poor souls who write to you, our new Dear Hattie. We don't want to break any hearts here, Peters. Do you understand?

ARTIE: Oh, yes, Ms. Johnson.

MS. JOHNSON: Good. Because yours is a job of great

responsibility. You hurt no one or else! Got it, Peters?

ARTIE: Got it, Ms. Johnson.

MS. JOHNSON: Good. And be certain to remember our motto: "If it's good news, it's our news."

ARTIE: Words to live by, Ms. Johnson.

MS. JOHNSON: *(As she exits)* Yes! And on our paper, those words are gospel!

ARTIE: *(After she's gone, sarcastically)* Be nice, be kind, be caring! Don't hurt anyone. Or she'll fire me! Ha! No one will ever fire me! I'm the best writer this paper has ever seen! And what business is it of hers that my girl friend thinks I'm fooling around with other girls? OK, so it's true! But Terry is such a baby. So sweet. It makes me sick! *(Reads letter.)* Another letter from a girl with a bad boy friend. Look at this. She's from Hoboken. That's where Terry lives. Mailed from a post office box number. I think Terry's father has one of those. A lot of people do. Anyway, let's see what this dingbat has to cry about. *(Reads sarcastically.)* Dear Hattie, I think my boy friend is cheating on me. I don't know what to do. I think he thinks I'm cheating on him, but I'm not. I love him. I want to marry him someday. He works so hard at his job. He's a newspaper man. And I do love him and don't want to lose him. What should I do? Signed, Heartbroken in Hoboken. *(Annoyed)* What a wimp! Ahhh, women! They're all alike! Pests! *(Puts paper in typewriter and types as light fades out on him and comes up on TERRY, who is Heartbroken in Hoboken.)* I'll tell her a thing or two. A wimp like that doesn't deserve a man.

TERRY: *(Reads)* Dear Heartbroken, all men are slime! So if I were you, I'd tell this two-timing creep you're so in love with to take a long walk on a short pier! Get rid of him! I, the loving Dear Hattie, an honest, caring, compassionate woman, can only say, drop this bozo like a hot potato! Remember, if men are not slime now, they will be shortly.

All the men I know are slime, why should yours be any different! So dump the jerk! Get a goldfish! Yours Compassionately, Dear Hattie. *(Angry)* Dear Hattie's right! All men are slime — and Artie Peters is no different! I'm dumping him right now! Cheat on me, will he? *(Checks her watch.)* He's still at work! I can catch him at the office! I'm glad he works right in the neighborhood. *(She exits running as fast as she can as light fades out on her.)*

ARTIE: *(As light comes up on him, pulls out typing paper from typewriter.)* **There. Another one bites the dust.** *(He laughs fiendishly as TERRY enters, but ARTIE doesn't see her yet.)* **Women! They're all slime! But then my woman — Terry — is so beautiful.** *(TERRY smiles.)* **I am crazy about her bod! True, she's no rocket scientist** *(TERRY is really annoyed at this)* **— but who cares about her brain?** *(TERRY comes up behind him and taps him on the shoulder, he turns and jumps up.)* **Terry! What are you doing here?**

TERRY: I'm dumping you, Arthur Peters, you creep!

ARTIE: But why?

TERRY: All men are slime! And you're no different!

ARTIE: Who told you that?!

TERRY: *(Points to Dear Hattie's portrait.)* **She did. The kind and compassionate Dear Hattie. Hey, what are you doing in Dear Hattie's office?**

ARTIE: Er . . . ummm . . . *(MS. JOHNSON enters.)*

MS. JOHNSON: *(Furious)* **Peters!**

ARTIE: *(Jumps, scared)* **Y-yes, Ms. Johnson?**

MS. JOHNSON: I was just told our switchboard is lighting up with complaints from our readers! They want to know what happened to Dear Hattie? They think she's gone psycho — as in chain saw massacre psycho! What have you been writing?!

TERRY: *(To ARTIE)* **You're Dear Hattie?!** *(To MS. JOHNSON)* **He said all men are slime!**

MS. JOHNSON: Who are you, young lady?

TERRY: *(Shows MS. JOHNSON the letter.)* **Heartbroken in Hoboken.**

MS. JOHNSON: *(Looks at letter, then, after reading it, is furious.)* **Peters! You wrote this?!**

ARTIE: *(Scared, trying to hide behind TERRY)* **Y-yes. You think it's too strong?**

MS. JOHNSON: *Strong?!* **I think it's slime! And you're slime, Peters! Pack up! You're through!**

ARTIE: **Through?**

MS. JOHNSON: **Fired! Get out!**

ARTIE: *(Picks up his typewriter, then to TERRY)* **I'll see you later, Terry?**

TERRY: **Not a chance! We're through, Artie Peters!** *(ARTIE exits sadly, head down.)*

MS. JOHNSON: **Good riddance! Now, what are we going to do to replace our dear, departed Dear Hattie?**

TERRY: **Dear Hattie? She's dead?**

MS. JOHNSON: **Shush. Don't tell anyone. Her public would be crushed. They all loved her so much.**

TERRY: **I know. So did I. I never missed one of her columns. I used to read all of them, and her books. I even collected all her old columns. Gee whiz, I have all her old reply letters memorized.**

MS. JOHNSON: **You do?**

TERRY: **I do. I'm even studying journalism at school. Someday, I want to help people like Dear Hattie always does — or did. I'm going to really miss her.**

MS. JOHNSON: **Studying journalism are you?** *(TERRY nods.)* **Well, how would you like a job?**

TERRY: **A job?**

MS. JOHNSON: **Yes. We just happen to need a kind, caring, person like you. Would you like to be the new Dear Hattie?**

TERRY: **Me?! Oh, yes!**

MS. JOHNSON: **Can you type?**

TERRY: **Eighty words per minute.**

MS. JOHNSON: Terrific! You're hired! *(Shakes TERRY's hand.)* **I'm glad to meet the new Dear Hattie.**

TERRY: Signed, Happy in Hoboken!

MS. JOHNSON: Right! *(Curtain falls as they gaze lovingly at portrait of Dear Hattie.)*

Someone for Everyone

PRODUCTION NOTES

PLAYERS: Announcer (male or female); 3 males; 5 females; extras for couples at dance.

PLAYING TIME: About 15 minutes.

COSTUMES: Dresses for JANE, MILLIE and SANDRA. BOB and DARLA in filthy overalls. BIFFO in funny clown costume with big red nose. CINDY in mime costume.

PROPERTIES: Horn, forms, files, water squirting rose, prop dead fish, trick hand buzzer that fits in palm, endless colorful silk handkerchief, kitten.

LIGHTING EFFECTS: The lights can dim out.

SOUND EFFECTS: Doorbell, romantic dance music.

Someone for Everyone

CHARACTERS: ANNOUNCER, for the opening setting and middle time passage; MILLIE, owner of the Someone for Everyone Dating Service; JANE, her potential business partner; BOB GLOB, a slob; SANDRA SHARP, a perfectionist; BIFFO, a clown; DARLA DUMPER, a sanitation worker; ERNEST EXACTO, an efficiency expert; CINDY, a mime; EXTRAS, couples at dance.

TIME: Today.

SETTING: Basic office with desk Center Stage. Chairs on left side, chair on right side of desk (on wheels). Filing cabinets (on wheels) against backdrop.

ANNOUNCER: *(Out front of curtain)* **Is there no hope for the lonely ones — the good but unpopular people called nerds, globs, slobs and turkeys — the offbeat and irregular among us? Yes, there is. Let me take you to the Someone for Everyone Dating Service — where you find a date or your money back.**

AT RISE: MILLIE and JANE enter.

JANE: **I don't know, Millie. I just don't know. You have a wonderful office.** *(Looks around.)* **And it's great that you started your own business. But I'm still pretty skeptical about all this, especially about becoming a business partner in a dating service. I can't see my investment paying off. I know I've always been a skeptic, but that's me.**

MILLIE: **Right. But why have you always been so skeptical, Jane?**

JANE: **I can't help it. It's just my nature, I guess.**

MILLIE: **On the contrary. Anyone can change! And I see**

you as someone willing to take a chance.

JANE: Me?

MILLIE: Yes, you. You've always been right out there, on the cutting edge. You may be a skeptic, but you're very independent and you would make a great entrepreneur.

JANE: Me? The world's biggest skeptic?

MILLIE: Right, you. Jane, I'm telling you this business is going to be a success. And I want you to work with me. Will you?

JANE: I'm not sure. *(Looking around)* And if you ask me, you can't possibly find a date for every client who comes in here.

MILLIE: Yes, I can. I just can't help but believe that out there there is someone for everyone.

JANE: But if I were to become your partner, I could go broke on your money-back guarantee.

MILLIE: I don't think so. I really don't. *(Goes to filing cabinet and pulls out a few files.)* Just look at these files. There are all sorts of people in here.

JANE: *(Looking at files)* But some are so . . . so obnoxious, or unattractive, or weird.

MILLIE: To you — maybe even to me. But I still believe there is someone for everyone out there — and it is my mission in life to bring those lonely people together. Everyone needs someone.

JANE: Even the nerds?

MILLIE: *(Putting files away)* Yes, even the nerds.

JANE: I don't know.

MILLIE: Well, I do. *(Checks her watch.)* As a matter of fact, I have an appointment right now with a client.

JANE: Who?

MILLIE: A Mr. Bob Glob. *(Doorbell rings.)* That's probably him now.

JANE: I hope he's handsome. *(BOB GLOB enters. He is a slob and JANE is disgusted by him, but MILLIE is polite. JANE whispers to MILLIE.)* **I hope he's human.**

MILLIE: *(Shaking BOB GLOB's filthy hand, she now has grease on her hand, but tries to keep smiling.)* **Hello. You must be Mr. Glob.**

BOB: **Yeah, that's me.** *(Scratches his head and shakes the sawdust out of it. JANE sneezes.)* **Bless ya!**

JANE: **Thank you.**

BOB: **Ya welcome. So who are you gals?** *(Pointing to JANE)* **She my date?**

JANE: *(Backs away a bit.)* **No, no!**

BOB: **So who are you?**

MILLIE: **I'm Millie, the owner of Someone for Everyone Dating Service, and this is my new associate, Jane. Have a seat.** *(They all sit.)*

BOB: **Terrific. So I hear you gals can find a date for anyone. Can you find me a date?**

MILLIE: **Yes. We believe that out there there is someone for everyone. Right, Jane?**

JANE: *(Looking at BOB)* **Er ... well ...** *(MILLIE kicks her in shin.)* **Yes! Right. Definitely.**

BOB: **Good. Because I just can't seem to find any gals who want to go out with me. Heck, I can't see why not. Can you?**

JANE: **Well, Bob ...** *(Holds her nose.)* **I seem to detect one reason.** *(She fans the air.)*

BOB: **Yeah? What's that?**

JANE: **You —**

MILLIE: *(Cutting JANE off)* **Are unique.**

BOB: **I know I smell a bit, but in my line of work, it ain't easy getting rid of the smell of fish guts. Fish are my life.** *(Pulls a dead fish out of his pocket.)* **See what I mean? But I never thought it would turn the ladies off.**

MILLIE: **Bob, to someone out there, you're perfect, unique.**

BOB: **Really?**

JANE: **Oh, yes. I can smell it in the air. You are unique.**

BOB: I am?

JANE: I'm positive. There is definitely only one of you. Maybe you're too unique.

BOB: See. I knew it! There's no one out there for me. No one!

MILLIE: Nonsense! I can find you someone you'll love.

BOB: Yeah. But will she love me? I know I'm a nice guy. I'm sensitive. I like fish.

JANE: Really? I'd never believe it.

BOB: It's true. I even love pets like rats and skunks. Did you know that dogs and cats actually follow me all over the city?

JANE: *(Holding her nose)* I wonder why.

BOB: Beats me.

MILLIE: It's because they like you, Bob. You have to have more self-confidence.

BOB: So you think cats and dogs like me?

JANE: I'm positive.

BOB: I guess you're right. Animals like me. But no one, especially gals, seems to see my sensitivity. I do have a good heart, you know. It's as big as a whale's. Can you find someone for me to love, Millie?

MILLIE: I guarantee it! *(JANE is slightly upset at this.)* Just fill out this form and mail it back to me. We're having a dance next month and all our matches will meet there. OK?

BOB: Sure. I can't spell too good. But *(Looking at form)* I can fill this sucker out. *(Gets up.)* See you gals at the dance. *(He exits.)*

JANE: Millie! How can you promise to find a date for that slob?

MILLIE: Jane, don't be so harsh. He seems like a nice guy.

JANE: But he smells like dead fish! What girl would ever want to go out with him? Maybe a mermaid, but not any human female.

MILLIE: Relax. I already have someone in mind. She's perfect.

– 131 –

JANE: I hope she owns a gas mask and a dust bin! *(Doorbell rings.)*

MILLIE: There's our next client. I believe her name is Sandra Sharp. She's a perfectionist or something. *(SANDRA enters. She is perfect.)*

SANDRA: Hello. I'm Sandra Sharp.

MILLIE: Have a seat, Ms. Sharp. I'm Millie, and this is my associate, Jane.

JANE: *(JANE whispers to MILLIE.)* She's perfect!

SANDRA: Can you help me? Or am I too perfect even for you?

MILLIE: No.

SANDRA: Good. Because, you see, I just can't seem to find a man who's willing to put up with me. I'm just too perfect, I guess.

JANE: I can see that. I'm sure we have dozens of guys who'd want to date you. Are you a model?

SANDRA: No. I was just born this way. Perfect. And with these looks, well, I just have to dress perfectly. Every button is always in its proper place. Colors must be perfectly coordinated. See this lipstick?

MILLIE: Yes.

JANE: What color is it?

SANDRA: The perfect color for this perfect dress.

JANE: Why do you think guys wouldn't want to go out with you?

SANDRA: Oh, they *all* want to go out with me. How could they not? I'm perfect. But unfortunately none of them wants to marry me. You know why?

MILLIE: Why?

SANDRA: They say I take too long to dress.

JANE: What? An hour?

SANDRA: I wish.

MILLIE: Two hours?

SANDRA: Try seven hours. And that doesn't include doing my hair or nails, which, of course, have to be perfect. So the guys get tired of waiting. A few fall asleep. Then they're gone. I know I'm perfect, but still I'm so lonely. Can you help me? Find me a nice guy?

MILLIE: I'm sure we can. *(Hands her a form.)* **Just fill this out. You'll be invited to our next match-up dance. It's next month. OK?**

SANDRA: *(Taking form)* **OK. I'll return it right away.** *(They stand.)* **Bye.**

JANE and MILLIE: **Bye.** *(SANDRA exits.)*

JANE: **You really think you can find a guy for Ms. Perfect?**

MILLIE: **You bet. Out there —**

JANE: **I know, I know. Out there there's someone for everyone.**

MILLIE: **Exactly! I guarantee it.** *(Doorbell rings.)* **That must be our next client. Biffo.**

JANE: **Biffo? You mean Biffo the Clown?**

MILLIE: **Right. You know him?**

JANE: **He's the funniest guy in the circus! He's world famous. He's made millions laugh. Who can forget his famous greeting.** *(In high-pitched clown's voice)* **"Hi, kids! What time is it? That's right! It's Biffo the Clown Time!"** *(In her voice)* **I love him.**

MILLIE: **Would you like to date him?**

JANE: **What? No way! Me dating a clown? What would everyone think? No way!**

BIFFO: *(BIFFO enters.)* **It's Biffo!** *(Shaking his own hand)* **Hello, hello. It's Biffo time!** *(MILLIE jumps as BIFFO honks his horn.)* **Oh, oh, you weren't ready for fun time, Millie?**

MILLIE: **Biffo, you've come in your make-up.**

BIFFO: *(Very sad)* **No. This is the real Biffo — big red nose and all.**

JANE: **Oh, boy.** *(Backs away a bit.)* **Well . . . hello anyway.**

BIFFO: **Hi.**

MILLIE: *(Shakes his hand and she jumps from hand buzzer.)* **Very happy to meet you.** *(BIFFO nods sadly.)*

JANE: What's wrong, Biffo?

BIFFO: No one loves me. *(Tears squirt out of his eyes.)*

JANE: Ahhh. Don't cry.

BIFFO: *(Wiping a tear with endless colorful silk handkerchief)* Sorry.

MILLIE: *(Pats him on back.)* That's OK, Biffo. Have a seat. And just remember, you have millions of fans who love you. *(They all sit.)*

BIFFO: But they all laugh at me! They all think I'm funny!

JANE: But you're a clown! You're supposed to be funny!

MILLIE: Right, Biffo.

BIFFO: Is it my fault that I'm a clown? Every girl I meet just can't keep a straight face.

JANE: *(Trying not to laugh)* I can't see why not.

BIFFO: *(Takes out his horn and beeps it; JANE laughs.)* See? I take out my horn and beep it and everyone laughs!

MILLIE: Biffo, we all know you're a very nice man under all that make-up.

BIFFO: Make-up? Make-up?

JANE: Your clown make-up.

BIFFO: What clown make-up?

MILLIE: The make-up you're wearing right now.

BIFFO: This isn't make-up. This is the real me!

JANE and MILLIE: What?!

BIFFO: Yes! I was born this way. Big red nose and all.

JANE: *(Looking at MILLIE)* He's a real clown.

BIFFO: Yes! I'm a real clown! Even she hates me!

MILLIE: No. Jane likes you.

JANE: *(Sarcastically to MILLIE)* Millie, do we have a date for a real clown? Hmmm?

MILLIE: *(Thinking)* Well . . .

BIFFO: Do you? I know I look different and all. But I am a nice person. I love little kids, and they love me. I'm sure I'd make a wonderful father.

MILLIE: So am I, Biffo.

BIFFO: So you think you can find me a nice girl who'll see the real me under all this? And who won't make fun of me, say mean things about my big red nose? *(JANE is trying not to laugh.)*

MILLIE: I'm sure we can. *(Hands BIFFO form.)* Just fill this out and return it. You'll then be invited to our match-up dance next month. Is that all right with you?

BIFFO: *(They all stand.)* Yes. Thank you.

MILLIE: *(To BIFFO as he exits)* You're welcome. And just remember, Biffo, out there there is someone for everyone. *(BIFFO nods and exits.)*

JANE: I just hope you're right, Millie. Who in the world would want to marry a clown?

MILLIE: Oh, don't you worry. I have someone perfect in mind for Biffo. But we'd better get to work matching up some of our other clients. We have our big dance coming up and we must be ready. *(As lights fade briefly, stagehands roll out desk and filing cabinet. The chairs can stay.)*

ANNOUNCER: The match-ups were accomplished. And now two weeks later, the moment of truth — do they go together? You decide.

(Many couples are dancing together as the lights come up with the sound of romantic music. MILLIE and JANE enter.)

JANE: *(Music fades.)* Well, I am amazed. You've certainly found a lot of matches. But where is Biffo, Sandra and Bob the Slob?

MILLIE: You mean Bob Glob.

JANE: Right, Mr. Slob, and Sandra Ms. Perfect and Biffo the Clown? Where are they and their matches?

MILLIE: I will confess, they were harder to find matches for, but I have and they should be arriving shortly. *(Sees BOB.)* In fact, here's Bob now. *(BOB enters; everyone fans the air or holds their noses and backs away from him.)*

BOB: *(Burps)* So where's that gal you promised me? *(Looks around at all the pretty girls, to one girl)* You her? *(Girl backs away.)* **You?** *(Another girl backs away; to MILLIE)* **Where is she? She here yet?** *(JANE backs away as she fans the air.)*

MILLIE: *(Smiling)* **As a matter of fact, Bob, here she comes now.** *(DARLA enters carrying a kitten; BOB smiles.)* **Bob, I'd like to introduce Darla Dumper.**

BOB: **She's ... she's perfect! And cats love her, too!**

DARLA: *(Petting kitten)* **Yeah. This little guy was following me around. Cats love me.**

BOB: **I can believe it! She's just like me!**

JANE: *(Still fanning air)* **Even the perfume is the same.**

DARLA: **So how's it going, Bob?**

BOB: **Great!** *(Closer to DARLA)* **So do I turn you on or what?** *(Does a pose.)*

DARLA: **You look like garbage! Fortunately, garbage is my first love. I'm a sanitation engineer.**

JANE: **A garbage man?**

DARLA: **A garbage person!**

MILLIE: *(To DARLA and BOB)* **So what do you two think?**

DARLA and BOB: **The chemistry is perfect!** *(They dance off as a new song starts.)*

JANE: **If that's chemistry, it must be Drano℠!**

MILLIE: **Who are we to judge? It's only important that they're happy.**

JANE: **I guess so. But what about Sandra and Biffo?**

MILLIE: **Here's Sandra now.** *(SANDRA enters.)*

SANDRA: **Sorry if I'm a bit late. But I started dressing this morning and I just finished. How do I look? Perfect?**

MILLIE: **You look fine, Sandra.**

SANDRA: *(Anxious)* **Just fine? Not perfect!**

JANE: **You're perfect. I hate you.**

SANDRA: **I know. Everyone is so jealous. Is it my fault that I look perfect? I try to look ordinary, but it's no use. I am just what I am — perfect.**

MILLIE: **You look fine —** *(SANDRA frowns.)* **I mean perfect!**

SANDRA: **I try. So where's my date? I'm so lonely. I need a** nice neat guy. He must be perfect! Then we'll both be perfect! Does such a man exist?

JANE: I'm not sure a human being like that exists.

MILLIE: Sure he does. And here he comes now. *(ERNEST enters.)* Sandra Sharp, I'd like to introduce your date, Ernest Exacto.

SANDRA and ERNEST: *(Looking each other over)* I can't believe it! You're perfect!

ERNEST: So what do you do, Sandra?

SANDRA: My nails, my hair. It's a dirty job, but I simply have to do it. Perfection is my life.

ERNEST: Mine, too!

SANDRA: No! You're kidding?

ERNEST: No, I'm not. I simply live for perfection.

SANDRA: Really?

ERNEST: Yes. I'm an efficiency expert. To me everything must be absolutely perfect.

SANDRA: And I am!

ERNEST: I can see that.

SANDRA: Oh, Ernie, I'm so happy!

ERNEST: Me, too. Thanks, Millie.

SANDRA: Yes, thanks. He's perfect.

MILLIE: You're perfect together.

JANE: The perfect couple. *(Aside)* I may throw up. *(SANDRA and ERNEST dance off.)* OK, OK, Millie. You lucked out on that one. But Biffo is a different story. He's a clown. Who'd ever want to date a clown?

MILLIE: You'd be surprised. Here's Biffo now. *(BIFFO enters.)*

BIFFO: Is she here yet, Millie? Will she mind my big red nose? Will she laugh at me?

MILLIE: I promise you, Biffo, she will never ever laugh at you.

JANE: Never ever?

MILLIE: Never ever.

BIFFO: I can't wait to meet her.

MILLIE: Ah, here she comes now. *(CINDY, a cute mime, enters. CINDY smiles at BIFFO.)* **Biffo the Clown, I'd like to introduce your date, Cindy the Mime.** *(They smile at each other and CINDY hands BIFFO a rose that squirts water in his face.)*

BIFFO: *(Laughing)* **She's perfect! Thank you, Cindy. I'll treasure this rose forever.** *(CINDY kisses BIFFO on the nose.)* **I love her already! I'm so happy!** *(CINDY smiles and does a happy dance.)*

JANE: Seems so is Cindy. *(CINDY nods.)*

MILLIE: I told you guys there was someone out there for everyone. *(BIFFO and CINDY hug MILLIE.)*

BIFFO: We thank you. *(CINDY and BIFFO hold hands and then dance.)*

MILLIE: I love my job. *(To JANE)* So you think you'll be working with me, Jane?

JANE: Yes. I was a bit skeptical.

MILLIE: A bit?

JANE: Well, very skeptical. But I can see now that you're amazing, Millie.

MILLIE: Thanks.

JANE: You're welcome. *(Thinks, watches everyone dancing, then)* By the way ... er ... do you think you can find a nice guy for this skeptical woman I know?

MILLIE: What woman?

JANE: Me!

MILLIE: Don't worry! I have the perfect guy for you! Don't forget —

JANE and MILLIE: *(Together)* Out there there's someone for everyone! *(They laugh as curtain falls.)*

LIGHT DRAMA

The Christmas Bandit

PRODUCTION NOTES

PLAYERS: 1 male, 2 females.

PLAYING TIME: About 13 minutes.

COSTUMES: Apron and casual clothes for BERNIE; MAXIE in police uniform; TOMMY in baggy jacket and ski mask.

PROPERTIES: Cash, 2 cups of coffee, sandwich, handcuffs, 3 pistols (one is a water pistol), pocket watch, bag with food.

SOUND EFFECTS: Church bells to sound Off-Stage to signal midnight and Christmas.

The Christmas Bandit

CHARACTERS: TOMMY, a poor bandit; BERNIE, deli owner; MAXIE, short for Maxine, a police woman.

TIME: Christmas Eve.

SETTING: BERNIE's deli. Backdrop has shelves with food, and holiday decorations, both for Chanukah and Christmas. There is a counter which BERNIE stands behind. A cash register is on one end of counter and coffee pot with hot coffee is on other end of counter. BERNIE wears an apron.

AT RISE: MAXIE is buying a sandwich and cup of coffee from BERNIE.

BERNIE: *(Handing MAXIE sandwich and cup of coffee)* **That's one pastrami on rye and one cup of hot coffee, black, no sugar. That it, Maxie?**

MAXIE: **That's it. How much do I owe you, Bernie?**

BERNIE: *(Waving MAXIE off)* **Forget it. It's Christmas time. And this is Christmas Eve. And here we are.**

MAXIE: **Yeah. Here we are. I'd rather be home with my kids, but Mommy's got to work, and she pulled this shift. So here I am.**

BERNIE: **Is it cold out there?**

MAXIE: **Freezing. This hot coffee sure hits the spot.**

BERNIE: **So is there much crime out there on Christmas Eve?**

MAXIE: **Yes and no. Not as much as usual, but enough for Christmas Eve.**

BERNIE: **Not all peace on earth or good will toward men, eh?**

MAXIE: **Nope. Or toward women for that matter. By the way, we've gotten the word from the precinct to be on the lookout for what they are calling the Christmas bandit. Seems every year we get someone or another needing some extra cash.**

BERNIE: To buy gifts for the kids?

MAXIE: *(A little laugh)* Yeah, sure. I wish that was all they'd buy. It would make our job a lot easier.

BERNIE: I guess life is rough for some folks.

MAXIE: Yeah, I guess so, Bernie. Well, I better hit the street. My break is over. Take care and have a Merry Christmas, and a Happy Chanukah, and watch out for any suspicious characters. This is not one of the nicer neighborhoods.

BERNIE: It's OK. But I'll watch out. *(Pulls out a pistol.)* Besides, I'm all ready for any desperadoes.

MAXIE: I see that. I'm glad you took my advice and got that pistol permit.

BERNIE: Yeah. I'm not crazy about guns. *(Puts pistol under counter.)* But a guy's got to be ready for anything these days.

MAXIE: Yep. Well, see you, Bernie. I'll be back in a little while, after I check out the block.

BERNIE: Bye. *(MAXIE exits as BERNIE cleans up the counter. Sings:)* Jingle bells, jingle bells, jingle all the way . . . Deck the halls with bounds . . . *(Thinks)* or is it bowers of holly? *(He hums Christmas carols and something for Chanukah as TOMMY enters. BERNIE's back is to TOMMY and BERNIE fixes shelves and decorations. He doesn't see or hear TOMMY, who wears a ski mask and takes out a pistol.)*

TOMMY: *(Coming up to counter and very nervous, talking in a deep voice, as if disguising it)* Stick 'em up!

BERNIE: *(Hands up, turns slowly.)* OK. They're up. Take it easy.

TOMMY: Shut up! This is a robbery!

BERNIE: Really? You mean you're not here for a pastrami on rye? A knish?

TOMMY: No. I'm here for bread!

BERNIE: We got white, rye, Italian, French.

TOMMY: Cut the jokes, old man! I'm talking about cash.

BERNIE: What? You have no sense of humor?

TOMMY: No. I can't afford it. I'm a serious bandit.

BERNIE: It's good to be serious. Especially if you have a gun, you know?

TOMMY: Yeah, yeah. So give me all your cash.

BERNIE: Can I lower my hands?

TOMMY: No. Get it with your teeth.

BERNIE: Huh? You serious?

TOMMY: No. That was a joke.

BERNIE: Oh. Very good. So you do have a sense of humor.

TOMMY: Yeah, yeah. I tried stand-up comedy once, but no one laughed.

BERNIE: Did you have the gun with you?

TOMMY: No. Why?

BERNIE: If you would have had the gun, maybe they would have laughed.

TOMMY: *(Puts gun in BERNIE's face.)* You laughing?

BERNIE: Nope. You're looking at Mr. Serious.

TOMMY: *(Pulls gun away.)* Good, because this is no joke. I'm robbing you. See?

BERNIE: Clear as a bell.

TOMMY: Really? You're not laughing at me?

BERNIE: A nervous giggle, maybe.

TOMMY: Look, old man —

BERNIE: Bernie. The name's Bernie.

TOMMY: OK, OK, Bernie, your money or your life.

BERNIE: *(Getting money out of cash register)* Not too original, but effective. *(Hands TOMMY money.)* Merry Christmas.

TOMMY: *(Takes money and counts it.)* Yeah, right. And a Happy New Year. Hey, there's only six bucks here.

BERNIE: It's Christmas Eve. We're not so busy.

TOMMY: Bull. *(Points gun at BERNIE.)* You're holding out on me!

BERNIE: No. No, I'm not. Everyone's home wrapping presents.

TOMMY: I don't have a home.

BERNIE: I don't have any presents.

TOMMY: Look, old man.

BERNIE: Bernie. Please.

TOMMY: Yeah, yeah, Bernie. *(Paces nervously.)* **All right, all right. So what are you doing here? Six bucks ain't worth turning on the lights in this dump.**

BERNIE: What? You want me to stay home alone on Christmas Eve?

TOMMY: **Alone? You got no family? But ... er —**

BERNIE: Wife died a few years ago and my kids live way on the other side of the country.

TOMMY: **Really? I didn't know.**

BERNIE: Why would you? I don't tell people anyway.

TOMMY: **Right. I wouldn't know.**

BERNIE: Right. So ... here I am. With the lox and the pastrami. And you. What's your name, kid?

TOMMY: *(Still in phony deep voice)* **Tom — hey, that's none of your business.**

BERNIE: So what are you going to buy with the six bucks?

TOMMY: **Well ...** *(Looks at money, thinks, then)* **Not much. I mean, what can you buy for six bucks these days?** *(TOMMY looks at food and coffee pot.)*

BERNIE: You hungry, kid?

TOMMY: **No.**

BERNIE: You sure you don't want a nice hot cup of coffee and a ham on rye?

TOMMY: **I have a gun!**

BERNIE: I have a bagel! You want a bagel? It's on the house.

TOMMY: **I have a gun.**

BERNIE: I know already. That's why it's on the house. If you didn't have a gun, I'd charge you. But since you're packing a rod, hey, it's on the house. Besides, you look like you could use a little food and drink. OK?

TOMMY: **Old man, this is a hold up. Stop trying to change the subject; stop trying to throw me off.**

BERNIE: Sorry. *(They are silent, then)* So ... you do this often? You don't seem so ... er ... professional.

– 145 –

TOMMY: Oh, no? Well, I do this a . . . a lot.

BERNIE: Could have fooled me.

TOMMY: I'm a professional! I do this every Christmas!

BERNIE: Oh, wait! You're that Christmas bandit Maxie told me about?

TOMMY: *(In deep voice)* No! That's a lie. *(Putting gun in BERNIE's face)* And who's this Maxie? Come on! Who's Maxie?

BERNIE: Er . . . just some dumb neighborhood kid. No one you'd know. Just a kid.

TOMMY: *(Taking gun out of BERNIE's face)* Good. Because if this Maxie was your partner or a cop . . .

BERNIE: What partner? This is my deli. I got no partner. You think this is Wall Street? This is a little deli. Bernie's little deli.

TOMMY: Good. Because if Maxie was a cop or a guy going to pop in here, you'd both end up shot dead. Got it?

BERNIE: Got it. You speak very clearly for a bandit with a ski mask on. You know how to make your point. I got it.

TOMMY: Good. *(Paces)*

BERNIE: Well, if that'll be all, I'd like to close up now.

TOMMY: Why? You got somewhere to go?

BERNIE: It is Christmas Eve.

TOMMY: I know that. You think I don't know that?

BERNIE: No. I'm sure you know it. So . . . no coffee then?

TOMMY: Well . . . yeah, yeah. But no funny business and no milk or sugar.

BERNIE: You got it. *(Gets coffee.)* No funny business and no milk or sugar.

TOMMY: Right, right.

BERNIE: Relax, kid. I'm not going to try anything. *(Hands TOMMY cup of coffee.)*

TOMMY: I . . . er . . . don't have any money.

BERNIE: It's on the house.

TOMMY: *(Hands BERNIE a dollar back.)* Here.

BERNIE: Thanks. *(Puts it in cash register.)* So you married?

TOMMY: Why do you want to know, old man?

BERNIE: You know old folks, always nosey.

TOMMY: Well, I'm married. But separated. OK?

BERNIE: Got any kids?

TOMMY: You are a nosey old coot.

BERNIE: Please. Call me Bernie. I hate "old man" and "old coot."

TOMMY: *(Nervously pacing)* Yeah, yeah. Bernie.

BERNIE: So do you have any kids?

TOMMY: Of course I have kids. Why do you think I do this? For myself?

BERNIE: Some do.

TOMMY: Well, I don't. I do it for my kids. And only on Christmas.

BERNIE: A seasonal bandit.

TOMMY: *(Sarcastically)* Right. I spend summers in Bermuda and Christmases here robbing two-bit delis.

BERNIE: Hey. This is not a two-bit deli. This is a good place. We carry all the essentials: bagels, lox, the Times, soda. This is a class operation, kiddo.

TOMMY: Sure, sure.

BERNIE: Hold it.

TOMMY: *(Scared, looks around, aims gun at BERNIE.)* What? Hold what?

BERNIE: Hey, easy kid. I just know it's got to be you.

TOMMY: I got to be who?

BERNIE: Yeah. I'm sure it's you. You're him.

TOMMY: Him? *(Putting gun in BERNIE's face)* Oh yeah? So who am I?

BERNIE: You really are that Christmas bandit. Right?

TOMMY: Is that what the cops are calling me?

BERNIE: Yep. So you're him. You're a lot smaller than I expected.

TOMMY: Hey, no height jokes. *(Sorry for doing this.)* Look, man, I'm sorry for robbing you. But my kids are hungry, you know? I can't get them the things they need. I try, but I can't get what they need.

BERNIE: You got a job?

TOMMY: I had one, then two, then three.

BERNIE: You keep losing them?

TOMMY: They keep firing me. They find out I'm an ex-con and fire me.

BERNIE: An ex-con? What were you in for?

TOMMY: Take a guess.

BERNIE: Armed robbery?

TOMMY: No! Whatever gave you that idea?

BERNIE: *(Shrugs)* Just a wild guess.

TOMMY: Well, I was sent up for helping to steal a car. My . . . er . . . wife had to go to the hospital, you know?

BERNIE: Sick, huh?

TOMMY: *(Still in phony deep voice)* She was going to have a baby. What was I to do?

BERNIE: Call a cab?

TOMMY: *(Thinks, then)* I guess I should have called a cab.

BERNIE: Yeah, or 911. *(They are silent, then)* So how'd you do tonight? Armed robbery-wise, I mean. You have enough to feed your kids?

TOMMY: I got five bucks.

BERNIE: You mean I'm your first robbery?

TOMMY: Yeah.

BERNIE: But then how come they call you the Christmas bandit? You'd have to have robbed more than one place.

TOMMY: You think I'm the only one doing this? Hey, old man, there are a lot of hungry kids out there with desperate parents. I'm not the only one. I'm not the only Christmas bandit.

BERNIE: I guess.

TOMMY: *(Puts empty cup of coffee on counter as MAXIE sneaks in behind TOMMY.)* Thanks for the coffee.

MAXIE: *(Puts gun in TOMMY's back.)* Freeze!

TOMMY: *(Hands up)* Don't shoot! I'm not armed!

BERNIE: Kid, what's that cannon you got?

TOMMY: My kid's water pistol.

MAXIE: *(Takes gun and sees how light it is, tries it.)* **It is a water pistol.** *(Gives gun to BERNIE, then to TOMMY)* **You're under arrest.** *(Hands water pistol to TOMMY, pulls off TOMMY's ski mask and we discover TOMMY is a young woman.)* **It's a girl!**

TOMMY: *(In her real voice)* **I'm a woman!**

BERNIE: Tomasina? It's you?

TOMMY: *(Head down)* **Yeah. Sorry, Bernie.**

MAXIE: *(To BERNIE)* **You know this girl?**

TOMMY: Woman, woman.

BERNIE: Yeah. She's one of my best customers, when she has money. I've known Tommy, Tomasina, since she was a little kid.

MAXIE: Wonderful. *(To TOMMY)* **You have the right to remain silent. Anything you say can and will be used against you. You have the right to an attorney; if you can't afford one, one will be appointed for you. Got it?**

TOMMY: Yeah, yeah. *(MAXIE turns TOMMY around, makes her put hands behind back, spreads her legs and frisks her.)*

MAXIE: *(Puts handcuffs on TOMMY after frisking her.)* **Good. Did she hurt you, Bernie?**

BERNIE: No, no. I'm fine.

MAXIE: Good.

TOMMY: So where you taking me?

MAXIE: To jail. Where do you think? *(Church bells ring.)*

BERNIE: *(Checks his pocket watch.)* **It's Christmas.**

MAXIE: Merry Christmas, Bernie.

BERNIE: Merry Christmas, Maxie. Merry Christmas, Tommy.

TOMMY: Yeah, yeah.

BERNIE: So you taking her in?

MAXIE: Yep. It's jail for this grinch.

TOMMY: My kids are going to go hungry.

MAXIE: You should have thought of that before you decided to stick people up, young lady.

BERNIE: Look, Maxine, let me pack a few things for her kids. It is Christmas.

MAXIE: Bernie, she tried to rob you.

BERNIE: Yeah, yeah. But her kids. No one should be hungry, especially on Christmas. *(Packs a bag with food.)* **We can drop this off at her apartment before we take her to the police station. OK, Maxie?** *(MAXIE thinks.)* **Please. Come on. It is Christmas.**

MAXIE: Geez, Bernie.

BERNIE: Please.

MAXIE: Yeah, yeah. OK. *(To TOMMY)* Girl, you got anything to say?

TOMMY: I'm sorry.

BERNIE: See? She's sorry.

MAXIE: That's what they all say when we catch 'em. Come on. Let's get going.

BERNIE: I'll just get my gun. *(He gets big gun.)*

TOMMY: You had a gun?

BERNIE: Yep.

TOMMY: You could have shot me. Why didn't you?

BERNIE: *(Shutting off lights, a little ironic)* It's Christmas.

TOMMY: *(Head down, sadly)* Yeah. Merry Christmas.

MAXIE: Right. Merry Christmas. You're lucky Bernie is a nice guy or you'd be leaving here another way, girl. You know that?

TOMMY: Yeah.

MAXIE: Yeah is right. So Merry Christmas.

BERNIE: Er . . . Maxie, one other thing.

MAXIE: Yeah, what's that, Bernie?

BERNIE: You can tell 'em down at headquarters that I'm not pressing charges.

TOMMY and MAXIE: You're not?!

BERNIE: Not this time. After all, it is Christmas.

TOMMY: Oh, Bernie. Merry Christmas. *(As they start to exit.)*

MAXIE: Yeah. I guess. Merry Christmas.

BERNIE: And peace on earth, good will toward men.

TOMMY and MAXIE: And women.

BERNIE: Right. *(They exit as curtain falls.)*

My Father?

PRODUCTION NOTES

PLAYERS: 2 males.

PLAYING TIME: 16 minutes.

COSTUMES: OLD JACK's hair is grey. He's in jeans and T-shirt. JOHN wears jeans and sports jacket.

PROPERTIES: Road map, fishing pole, bait, 2 photographs.

LIGHTING EFFECTS: Moonlight.

SOUND EFFECTS: Sound of loud spashes from Offstage.

SPECIAL EFFECTS: When OLD JACK and JOHN are Offstage, they can stand in a large basin and be wet down with water so they appear to have been in bay.

My Father?

CHARACTERS: OLD JACK SIMPSON, owner of run-down clam bar; JOHN JOHNSON, OLD JACK's biological son whom he hasn't seen since JOHN was a baby.

TIME: Evening.
SETTING: The dock of OLD JACK's Clam House. A sign saying that sits over backdrop of little run-down, bay side, roadside clam bar.
AT RISE: OLD JACK sits at edge of stage, as if on edge of his dock. He is fishing.

OLD JACK: *(Pulling in empty line, which he baits)* **Nothing. The story of my life. Stole my bait, too. Great. So what else is new? You work all your life and still no brass ring. And this place. Old Jack's Clam House. Between the taxes and the electric bills . . .** *(JOHN enters; OLD JACK doesn't see him. JOHN looks at his map and then at a photo. He stuffs map in back pocket. He smiles and walks over to OLD JACK.)*

JOHN: **Jack? Jack Simpson?**

OLD JACK: **That's me, kid. Old Jack Simpson. That's what they call me around these parts. What can I do for you?**

JOHN: **You know who I am?**

OLD JACK: *(Looking at JOHN)* **A tax collector?**

JOHN: **Me? No.**

OLD JACK: **You're from the health department? What? Some city slicker complaining again about ptomaine poisoning? That's bull. I run a clean place. There's no ptomaine here. You are from the health department, aren't you?**

JOHN: **No. No, I'm not.**

OLD JACK: **Wrong again, huh? The story of my life. You sure look like a tax collector or someone from the health department.**

JOHN: No, sorry. You're wrong again.

OLD JACK: So what else is new? You're not from the electric company then? You're not going to turn off my lights and oven, are you?

JOHN: No, no. My name's Johnson.

OLD JACK: Hello, Johnson. My name's Simpson. Jack Simpson.

JOHN: I know.

OLD JACK: You know? Oh, yeah, right. So then who are you? From the I.R.S.? Tell the truth. You're really from the I.R.S.

JOHN: No. No, really, I'm not.

OLD JACK: Then who the heck are you? And what can I do for you? You want to sit a while here on my dock? Fish? I got another rod and reel in the shack.

JOHN: *(Looks at "water" and steps back a bit.)* No. That's OK. I just want to talk to you.

OLD JACK: Yeah? About what? Oh, now I know who you are. You're that guy from the real estate place. You've come to make me an offer on my place.

JOHN: No. Why? *(Looks around at clam bar.)* You selling this place?

OLD JACK: Yup. Have to.

JOHN: Why? This beach is pretty popular for its seafood. You have a great location. And you can catch your clams right here, right off the dock.

OLD JACK: Not anymore I can't.

JOHN: Sure you can.

OLD JACK: No, I can't. The health department won't allow that. Water's polluted.

JOHN: Oh. But you're fishing.

OLD JACK: Sure I'm fishing. You think I believe some college kid from the stupid health department? No, I don't. But this fish is for me. You know? It's for me. Who said I have to believe the health department? I won't serve what I catch. So don't worry. *(Pulls in empty line.)* Great. Nothing.

JOHN: At least they didn't steal your bait.

OLD JACK: Thank the Lord for small favors.

JOHN: You catch much around here?

OLD JACK: No. Not today. Used to. But as you can see, not much lately. Think they all swam down to Florida, which is where I should be.

JOHN: So you eat what you catch?

OLD JACK: Saves money to eat what you catch. That is if I ever catch anything.

JOHN: You will if you just hang in there. The main thing about fishing is persistance. If you hang in there, you'll eventually catch that big one.

OLD JACK: Oh, yeah? Who told you that, kid?

JOHN: My father. Well, my adoptive father. He's a great guy.

OLD JACK: Sure. So he told you that about fishing?

JOHN: He taught me a lot of things. Like never to give up.

OLD JACK: I see. So your old man told you that fish story?

JOHN: My dad, well, not exactly my dad, but . . .

OLD JACK: But? But what? Did your dad tell you or what?

JOHN: Well, I thought he was my dad. Like I said, he adopted me after my mom remarried. He's not my real father.

OLD JACK: *(Looking at JOHN)* You thought he was? What are you talking about? I mean, he is or he isn't your father. Right?

JOHN: Sounds so simple the way you put it. But it's not.

OLD JACK: Oh, no? *(Pulls in line and lays rod down.)* Why not? You have a fight with your dad? Is that it?

JOHN: No, no. *(Sits on dock with OLD JACK.)* We're still close. We always will be. I mean, I love him and all. It's not important that he really isn't . . . isn't . . .

OLD JACK: He really isn't what?

JOHN: My father.

OLD JACK: Hold it. You telling me your father isn't your father?

JOHN: I said that. He adopted me. He's not my *real* father. Not my biological father.

OLD JACK: Oh, I get it. You were adopted.

JOHN: That's what I've been saying. *(Thinks)* But no. Not exactly.

OLD JACK: Here we go again. Then what? What are you saying? I mean, you were adopted or you weren't adopted. Right?

JOHN: Not exactly.

OLD JACK: Then your real father died? Your mom remarried this guy who may or may not be your real and/or adopted father?

JOHN: Yes and no.

OLD JACK: What is this, kid? Twenty questions? Yes and no. Not exactly? What are you talking about?

JOHN: My real father, my biological father, didn't die. But my mom did remarry.

OLD JACK: Good for your mom. So what'd her old man do? Dump her?

JOHN: *(Thinks)* I'm not sure.

OLD JACK: Well, neither am I. I'm just a clam digger. What are you telling me all this for?

JOHN: Because I think you're my father.

OLD JACK: *(Gets up and stares at JOHN for a few seconds.)* What?

JOHN: I said, I think you're my real dad, my biological father.

OLD JACK: Hold it, kid. Me? Your dad? You've got to be kidding.

JOHN: *(Shows old photo to OLD JACK.)* Isn't this you?

OLD JACK: *(Looking at photo)* Yeah. Where'd you get that? Off the wall of my clam house?

JOHN: No. From my mom. She finally told me about my real dad. About you.

OLD JACK: *(Gets up and walks about.)* Well, she lied. It ain't me. No way.

JOHN: She told me you ran away. You were out of work, and when you were working, you couldn't earn enough to support her and a baby. So you ran off. You told her she'd be better off without you. She'd be better off on welfare, you told her.

OLD JACK: *(Looks at JOHN, knowing he's right.)* Look, you have me mixed up with someone else.

JOHN: *(Holds up photo for OLD JACK to see.)* So this isn't your picture?

OLD JACK: Yeah, it's my picture, but so what? You could have gotten it anywhere.

JOHN: I got it from my mother.

OLD JACK: Come on, kid. Why don't you just go back to where you came from? I'm busy.

JOHN: Doing what? Fishing?

OLD JACK: I was just on my evening break. I'm a busy man. So take your picture, wherever you got it from, and go back home. OK? I'm busy.

JOHN: *(Stands)* That's not what I've heard.

OLD JACK: Oh, yeah? What have you heard? You been spying on me?

JOHN: No.

OLD JACK: I don't know why not. Everyone else is. Everyone from the telephone company to the I.R.S. They think I'm really rich. That I'm hiding my millions away, in some big sea chest like Captain Hook. Well, I'm not rich. I'm busted. So stop spying on me.

JOHN: I'm not. Really. I've been searching for you. All over. In the process, I've been finding out all sorts of things.

OLD JACK: Yeah? Like what?

JOHN: You're in debt for one. If you don't come up with some cold hard cash real soon, you're going to lose this place.

OLD JACK: No, I'm not. No one's going to take this gold mine away from Old Jack Simpson. Over my dead body.

JOHN: Maybe I can help you get this place back into shape.

OLD JACK: *(Looks at JOHN.)* Oh, yeah? Why?

JOHN: Why? Because you're my father.

OLD JACK: *(Wincing)* Geez! Kid, I wish you'd stop saying that. I'm not your father.

JOHN: You telling me you didn't run away from me and Mom when I was a baby?

OLD JACK: I'm telling you I'm not your father. *(Pause as JOHN thinks of what next to say.)* You want to go for a swim?

JOHN: No.

OLD JACK: *(Looking out over the audience)* It's a nice night for a swim. Full moon is up, the water's calm. It's summer. Why not?

JOHN: *(Afraid to admit he can't swim)* I . . . er . . . didn't bring my suit.

OLD JACK: It's just us, kid. Who needs a suit? But if you want one, I have an extra one in the place. Want it?

JOHN: No. I don't want to go swimming. I want to talk to you. Find out about you. Come on. Can't we talk?

OLD JACK: Kid, I've got nothing to say to you. It's hot and I want to go swimming. You coming or going?

JOHN: I can't swim.

OLD JACK: *(Laughing)* What? You can't swim?

JOHN: Come on. Stop laughing. It's not funny.

OLD JACK: Sorry, sorry. But it's sort of funny. I mean I know dogs that can swim, little babies. And you can't swim? A big guy like you?

JOHN: Look, I'm from the city, you know? I haven't had time to learn how to swim.

OLD JACK: Sure, sure. Excuses, excuses. You're just chicken. Afraid of the water.

JOHN: And you're afraid to admit you're my father.

OLD JACK: I'm going swimming. *(OLD JACK begins to take off his shirt.)* You coming or not? If you can't swim, I'll teach you.

JOHN: No thanks. I'll wait here.

OLD JACK: *(Sits down at edge of dock and JOHN sits beside him.)* Forget it. I can swim later. The night's young.

JOHN: Great. So tell me about yourself? How'd you find this great little place on the bay?

OLD JACK: I bought it from some old sea dog years ago. He was too old to keep it going. So I bought it for a steal.

JOHN: What happened to the old sea dog?

OLD JACK: *(Shrugs)* Hightailed it to Florida, I think. He's probably dead now. Like this place.

JOHN: I can help you fix it up. It could be a gold mine. You have plenty of traffic here.

OLD JACK: So why doesn't anyone stop?

JOHN: Why would they? This place doesn't even look like it's open.

OLD JACK: Well, it is.

JOHN: You sure don't advertise it. What are you doing? Hiding out?

OLD JACK: *(Thinks, then)* Listen, kid, I'm tired of talking. I just want to go swimming. Come on, I'll teach you.

JOHN: No. I hate the water.

OLD JACK: Oh, I get it. You're afraid you'll drown.

JOHN: I just don't like the water. I draw the line at the bathtub. Maybe, just maybe, a hot tub. *(Looking out over "water")* But not this. Not on the open sea.

OLD JACK: Open sea? This is just a nice little bay. Besides, if you hate the water so much, why do you want to help me fix up this place? It's right by the water. You forget that? You could come out here one night and fall off the dock. You don't know how to swim, you could drown.

JOHN: You're my father. I just want to help you.

OLD JACK: I'm not your father. Stop saying that.

JOHN: I have proof.

OLD JACK: Proof? What proof? That picture?

JOHN: More than that.

OLD JACK: Oh, yeah? Like what? Blood tests? DNA typing? I haven't had my DNA looked at in weeks. Besides, that's not totally for certain.

JOHN: Ninety-nine point eight per cent, they say.

OLD JACK: Sounds like Ivory™ soap. Ninety-nine and forty-four one hundreths per cent pure. Well, it ain't so pure and simple. Lab technicians make mistakes. Mix things up.

JOHN: *(Shows OLD JACK another photo.)* I have this.

OLD JACK: *(Looking at photo)* Me and Sandy.

JOHN: My mom. Know who that baby is?

OLD JACK: Let me guess. You?

JOHN: *(Taking photo back)* Right. This was taken just before you ran off.

OLD JACK: *(After some thought, looks away.)* Well . . . I did what I thought was best. OK?

JOHN: Best for who?

OLD JACK: You and your mom. If I left, it would be easier for her to get on welfare. So I left.

JOHN: You ran away. Like you're running away from here.

OLD JACK: No one is running away from anything. They're taking it away from me.

JOHN: Bull. You're letting them take it. What's wrong with you? Why do you keep running away? You afraid of responsibility? Commitment?

OLD JACK: What are you, kid? A shrink? That it? You go to shrink school?

JOHN: I'm a carpenter. I build houses. I can help you rebuild this place.

OLD JACK: Don't trouble yourself. It's a waste of time.

JOHN: What are you afraid of?

OLD JACK: Me? Afraid? And what about you? You're the one who's afraid of going for a little swim. Not me. What are you afraid of?

JOHN: Being afraid of the water is no big deal. It's not the same as being afraid of your responsibilities.

OLD JACK: Kid, leave me alone. I'm doing just fine. I don't need your help, or your psychological mumbo jumbo. Who do you think you are coming here and screwing up my life? Go home. Leave me alone. I was doing all right before you came along. *(Stands, takes off his shirt.)* And I'm hot so I'm going in for a swim. You coming, or are you afraid? Have no confidence in yourself?

JOHN: *(Stands)* You're the one who is afraid. You're the one who won't let me be a part of your life. You're the one who doesn't have any confidence in yourself. I'm going. I guess I made a mistake coming back here. Mom was right. You are a loser!

OLD JACK: She called me that?

JOHN: And a few other things.

OLD JACK: Sandy always had a way with words.

JOHN: Well, she was sure right about you. I'm leaving. Have a nice life. *(Begins to exit.)*

OLD JACK: Yeah, sure. You too, kid.

JOHN: The name's Jack!

OLD JACK: Jack?

JOHN: Yes! She named me after you! *(He exits.)*

OLD JACK: *(Sees something that frightens him)* Jackie, watch that loose plank there on the dock!

JOHN: *(From Offstage we hear a splash, then JOHN:)* Help! I can't swim!

OLD JACK: Relax, kid! I'm coming! *(OLD JACK runs off, we hear another splash. After a few moments, OLD JACK and JOHN re-enter. Both are soaking wet.)* You OK, son?

JOHN: *(Looks at OLD JACK.)* Yeah. You hear what you just called me?

OLD JACK: What?

JOHN: You called me son.

OLD JACK: It just came out. I didn't mean anything by it.

JOHN: I think you did. Thanks for saving me.

OLD JACK: Don't mention it. What were you doing there?

The dog paddle?

JOHN: Anything I could think of. I was scared.

OLD JACK: Yeah, I know what you mean. Scared me there for a second.

JOHN: You were afraid for me?

OLD JACK: *(Making up a story to cover his real feelings)* No. I figured if you drowned on my dock, I'd be sued. That's all I need. Then I'd really lose this place. But then again, as it is, if I don't come up real quick with some cold hard cash, as you put it, they are going to auction this place right out from under me.

JOHN: Let me help you. We can be partners.

OLD JACK: Partners? What is this? Wall Street? Partners? In this dump?

JOHN: Sure. Why not?

OLD JACK: You're a nut, kid.

JOHN: Come on. Let's give it a try, give it our best shot. What do you say? *(OLD JACK thinks.)* Come on. You know it's a good idea. I'll be your partner. We can make this place great again. Together.

OLD JACK: Nah. I'm going to Florida. I'll be like that old sea dog.

JOHN: Right. Die of old age while tanning your butt on some dumb beach. You like the sun that much?

OLD JACK: It sure beats battling with the I.R.S. and Ma Bell.

JOHN: Afraid of a little fight?

OLD JACK: Old Jack? No. No way.

JOHN: Good. Then let me help you fix this place up. Florida sun and fun isn't your style.

OLD JACK: No? It sure sounds nice when I see them commercials on TV.

JOHN: You'd die of boredom down there.

OLD JACK: Hey, don't knock it. As good a way of going than most.

JOHN: No. You're staying here with me and we're going to

make this place a show place by the bay.

OLD JACK: *(A laugh)* A show place by the bay ... *(Smiles)* You're a dreamer, kid.

JOHN: Someone has to be.

OLD JACK: Yeah, I guess. We all had our dreams once. Even me and your mom.

JOHN: So we can work together on this place. We can turn it into a real show place.

OLD JACK: I would like that.

JOHN: Then let me help you. I'm a great carpenter.

OLD JACK: But a lousy swimmer.

JOHN: Swimming isn't important.

OLD JACK: In the city swimming may not be important, kid — but out here by the water, it is. You never know when a plank is going to rot out from under you.

JOHN: Yeah, I guess you're right on that.

OLD JACK: Listen, kid.

JOHN: Jack.

OLD JACK: OK, OK. Jack. Thanks for your good intentions, but no thanks, if you know what I mean.

JOHN: Dad, listen.

OLD JACK: Don't do that.

JOHN: What?

OLD JACK: Call me that.

JOHN: What?

OLD JACK: Kid, you called me Dad.

JOHN: Well, you are my father.

OLD JACK: Just call me Old Jack. OK?

JOHN: This is going to be real confusing. Two Jacks.

OLD JACK: You're the one who's afraid of the water.

JOHN: And you're the one who's afraid of commitment.

OLD JACK: Yeah. *(Sits on edge of dock.)* Anything you say.

JOHN: Listen, I have a deal for you.

OLD JACK: Another one?

JOHN: Just listen. *(Sits on edge of dock.)*

OLD JACK: I'm all ears.

JOHN: OK. Here's the deal: you let me stay here awhile and help you put this place back into shape, and you can try to teach me how to swim. A deal?

OLD JACK: That could take a while.

JOHN: *(Looking the clam bar over)* Tell me about it. This place is in bad shape.

OLD JACK: *(A bit of irony)* What? Not my clam bar. *(Looks at it.)* Well, it could use a little work. *(Picks up fishing rod and rebaits hook and starts fishing.)*

JOHN: A little? We're talking major surgery here. It could take months.

OLD JACK: Actually, what I meant was that teaching you how to swim could take months. It could take a real long while. You're no Greg Louganis, Jackie boy. We could be at it for ages.

JOHN: Great. It'll give us time to get to know each other. OK? *(Puts his hand out to shake.)*

OLD JACK: Well ... *(Shakes JOHN's hand.)* What the heck, yeah, yeah.

JOHN: Great.

OLD JACK: But you have to promise to apply yourself. No chickening out. And dog paddling doesn't count. OK, son?

JOHN: *(Big smile as he shakes OLD JACK's hand firmly.)* Hey, no problem. OK. Great, Dad. It's a deal.

OLD JACK: *(Gets a bite on line, trying to pull in something big.)* Wow!

JOHN: What is it?

OLD JACK: I just hooked a whopper! *(Curtain falls as OLD JACK fights to pull in big fish.)*

The Artist's Model

PRODUCTION NOTES

PLAYERS: 1 male; 1 female.

PLAYING TIME: About 11 minutes.

COSTUMES: MARK in paint-spattered jeans, JANE in diaphanous gown.

PROPERTIES: Brush, palette, rags, paint.

LIGHTING EFFECTS: Natural.

SOUND EFFECTS: Beep beep of watch.

The Artist's Model

CHARACTERS: MARK, an artist; JANE, his model.

TIME: Afternoon.

SETTING: An artist's studio. Paintings of beautiful women and landscapes by famous artists hang on walls. MARK's paintings are piled against walls. A stool sits Stage Left and an easel with canvas sits Stage Right beside small table with paints, rags, brushes and artist's palette. We cannot see what MARK is painting.

AT RISE: JANE sits on stool as MARK picks up palette and brush and starts painting her.

JANE: **So, do you do this often?**

MARK: **Do I do what often?**

JANE: **Paint beautiful women.**

MARK: **Is that what I'm doing?**

JANE: **Isn't it?**

MARK: **What do you think?**

JANE: **I think you're painting me. Aren't you?**

MARK: **Yes. And you are beautiful?**

JANE: **So, do you do this a lot?**

MARK: **Sure. All the time. Look around my studio.** *(Points to paintings.)* **See them? Piled against the wall. My hope is to someday capture the beauty that all those great artists captured.**

JANE: *(Looking around)* **Yes. They are quite beautiful.**

MARK: **I know. And there are so many of them.**

JANE: **Yes. There are quite a few. And all such beautiful women.** *(She moves as if she feels upset, thinking she is not as beautiful as the women in these paintings.)*

MARK: **Yes. And beautiful landscapes.**

JANE: **What do you like painting more? Beautiful women or beautiful landscapes?**

– 166 –

MARK: Women. They at least talk to me.

JANE: Like I'm doing?

MARK: Yes.

JANE: And the land doesn't talk to you? *(She smiles.)*

MARK: Very good. Hold that smile. You have a smile like one of Titian's nudes.

JANE: Thank you, I think.

MARK: You're welcome, I'm sure.

JANE: The land doesn't talk to you?

MARK: In its own way it does.

JANE: It does? Ah-ha! And what does it say?

MARK: It says: I'm quiet, I'm warm, I'm full of life.

JANE: Sort of like a beautiful woman, eh?

MARK: Exactly. You give the feeling of hope, beauty, promise. All beautiful things do. A wonderful landscape. A colorful still life. Someone like you.

JANE: So, you paint to give the world hope, beauty?

MARK: And peace. But in a way, I do it to give me hope. When I see someone like you, with your smile, when I see the graceful way you move, the way you think and talk, I suddenly can live with all the bad things that happen in life.

JANE: I . . . do all that for you?

MARK: And more.

JANE: But I'm not really that beautiful, Mark. Most people would call me plain, ordinary, plain Jane. That's me.

MARK: That's not how I see you.

JANE: You're an artist. What do you know?

MARK: Truth and beauty. That's all there is and all you need to know — to quote the poet. To me you're the most beautiful woman in the world.

JANE: Oh, great. I've heard that line before.

MARK: But it's true.

JANE: Sure, sure.

MARK: To me it's the truth. You're truth and beauty. You're what the world needs more of. You exude goodness, sweetness.

JANE: Do you say that to all your models?

MARK: *(Shrugs)* In some ways, I guess I do. We often talk.

JANE: About what? Truth and beauty?

MARK: Not always. Most of them want to know if, now that I've painted them, if they're going to be famous someday. They want to know if they're going to hang in the Louvre like Mona Lisa and become a woman of mystery like her.

JANE: Do you think I'll ever hang in the Louvre?

MARK: See? I told you.

JANE: So, I'm just like all the others, huh?

MARK: That's OK.

JANE: It is? Why?

MARK: Because most people are the same inside.

JANE: Really? In what ways?

MARK: We all want to be remembered. We all want to hang in the Louvre, or in someone's memory. We all want to be thought of fondly by someone when we're gone. Either by family or friends.

JANE: Or the art historians?

MARK: Yeah. Right. I want to be remembered for trying to create something worth remembering. For bringing a little beauty and truth into the world. I want to leave something worthwhile behind.

JANE: And that's why you're painting landscapes and beautiful women? And me?

MARK: Yes, that is why I am painting you. Can you just tip your head a little to the side. *(She does.)* Yes, right. Just try to hold that.

JANE: So tell me more. What do you tell all these other women you've painted?

MARK: Tell them? What do you mean?

JANE: You know. Do you flirt with them, tell them they're beautiful? Do they flirt with you?

MARK: Why do you want to know?

JANE: Why? Let's just say I'm curious.

MARK: Yes, I can see that.

JANE: Well ... what do you tell them? Do you tell them they're beautiful?

MARK: I tell them the truth.

JANE: And what is that?

MARK: It's different for each of them.

JANE: I see. How is it different?

MARK: That depends on them. How they are. Everyone is different.

JANE: Tell me about it. Do any of them flirt with you?

MARK: They are only human.

JANE: Very funny. I see you have a sense of humor as well as a sense of truth.

MARK: You have to to be an artist these days. It's not like it was for the old masters. Back then there was no TV, no camcorders, no cinema verite. They — the painters, the sculptors — they were the truth, they were the ones who created the images that shaped the world of seeing.

JANE: And you?

MARK: Me? I have to compete with MTV and Kodak™ and Polaroid™. They have managed to capture far more truth and beauty in one week than I'll ever be able to capture in my whole life.

JANE: Yeah. Gee, doesn't that bother you? Make you feel so ... so inadequate?

MARK: All I feel is a need to create, to communicate. *(He shrugs.)* I do what I have to do. I paint. I have no choice. It's not just what I love to do. It's what I have to do. There is something inside me that just drives me on to do this silly thing called painting.

JANE: Silly? Why is it silly?

MARK: When you think of smearing oil and bits of colored pigment on a swatch of canvas stretched on a wooden frame, it seems almost primitive. I think back to those cave painters.

JANE: The ones from Altamira?

MARK: Exactly. What were those cave men —?

JANE: Or cave women?

MARK: True. We really don't know if those prehistoric paintings were done by men or women or both. But the big question is, what were those artists thinking when they painted those cave walls?

JANE: What do you think they were thinking?

MARK: I often wonder. Just what was going through those ancient minds when they were painting those images? And why did they do it?

JANE: I heard those cave paintings had a religious significance.

MARK: But in ways all art does.

JANE: Even paintings of beautiful women?

MARK: I only know why I paint. And it's a form of love, admiration for a subject, the hope to capture it for all to see and for all to gain something good from. To uplift, to bring hope. In ways, isn't that what those ancient cave painters and all those old masters were after?

JANE: Maybe. But to get back to the real world.

MARK: What? Why? *(Checks his watch.)* Is it lunch time already?

JANE: No, not yet. I just meant, do you flirt with your models?

MARK: Am I flirting with you?

JANE: That's not what I asked. *(Pause, then)* OK, then, do any of your models flirt with you?

MARK: What do you think?

JANE: I think they probably do.

MARK: You do?

JANE: Yes. I do. They are only human. Like me.

MARK: Yes. And that's why I paint them.

JANE: I know. And that's what makes a model wonder. You artists must always be in love.

MARK: *(He laughs.)* You think so?

JANE: I do. You're all so passionate.

MARK: About beautiful sunsets? Or just about beautiful women?

JANE: About everything! You have such ... drive. Don't you ever get frustrated?

MARK: All the time.

JANE: But why? You seem so lucky. You're so talented. You create such beautiful paintings that everyone loves. What more can you ask for?

MARK: The ability to create without effort?

JANE: But you make it seem so easy, the way you paint.

MARK: Anyone can learn the basic techniques of putting paint on canvas. But the ability to create a work of art — men and women can go through their whole life striving for that. And what is so frustrating is that you never really know if you've done it.

JANE: You can't tell if you've created a masterpiece?

MARK: No. Do you think da Vinci had any idea that the Mona Lisa would become his masterpiece, or that the ceiling of the Sistine Chapel would become Michelangelo's? You just can never tell. So you keep trying. You keep working. You keep striving for that dream you just can't seem to catch up to or leave behind. So you keep moving, doing.

JANE: And so I'm just one beautiful woman somewhere in the middle of a long line of beautiful women who someday might be remembered by the world? Who might someday be hanging in the Louvre? Who might someday become your masterpiece?

MARK: I should be so lucky.

JANE: Do you're models ever fall in love with you?

MARK: Why do you ask?

JANE: Very funny. I ask because I'm falling in love with you.

MARK: Again? Janie, you say that every time I paint you. Every time we talk like this.

JANE: I know, I know. But I can't help it. I love doing this.

MARK: So do I.

JANE: You know, the thing I love about you the most is your unshakable belief that all this matters. That you can make a difference, that you can do it.

MARK: I do try.

JANE: And you never give up. So be honest. Tell me the truth. Do all your models fall in love with you?

MARK: Some do. But I already have someone I love.

JANE: (She smiles.) I know. And does she love you?

MARK: She tells me she does.

JANE: Oh, yeah? She just tells you? Does she ever show you?

MARK: In her way.

JANE: Really? In what way?

MARK: By the way she puts up with me. Painters are not the happiest people. They can be pretty miserable at times, especially when they're trying to capture an image that seems so elusive.

JANE: Like me?

MARK: (He smiles.) Like you.

JANE: I see. So this woman you love manages to put up with you, eh?

MARK: She does. For a few years now. And every day I love her more and more.

JANE: (She smiles.) Really?

MARK: Really. She makes all this worthwhile. In ways, I think it's *her* beauty, *her* love, I keep trying to capture. The essence of what she gives to me.

JANE: Her love, eh?

MARK: That's what I said. But it's more than just love. It's her friendship, her truth, her goodness.

JANE: Maybe it's your love for her that keeps driving you.

MARK: Isn't that what I just said?

JANE: No, you said it was her love for you.

MARK: Oh. Well ... I know it has something to do with love.

JANE: Which is why I keep wondering if all these other

models you paint are in love with you.

MARK: **Maybe they are.**

JANE: **And maybe they aren't?**

MARK: **No. Maybe I'm not in love with them.**

JANE: **You're not?**

MARK: *(Alarm goes off, MARK checks his watch and turns off alarm on it.)* **God. Look at the time.**

JANE: **Time already?**

MARK: **Yep. Time to pick up the kids at nursery school.**

JANE: **Right. I almost forgot.**

MARK: **I know.**

JANE: *(Comes over and hugs MARK and they kiss passionately.)* **It's just that I love you so much.**

MARK: **I know that.**

JANE: **You do, do you?**

MARK: **Of course I do. And that's why I married you and why we are living happily ever after and why we better get cleaned up, dressed and moving, because the kids are waiting for us at nursery school.**

JANE: *(Smiles)* **Yeah. Our two little masterpieces.**

MARK: **You got that right.** *(They exit arm in arm as curtain falls.)*

Too Old to Dance

PRODUCTION NOTES

PLAYERS: 4 females; 1 male.

PLAYING TIME: About 12 minutes.

COSTUMES: The women in leotards; MIKA in tights and baggy sweatshirt.

PROPERTIES: Gear bags, sheet music.

SOUND EFFECTS: Ballet music from on-stage record player.

Too Old to Dance

CHARACTERS: SUSAN, oldest dancer; TAMI, younger dancer; MARLI, younger dancer; BARBARA, youngest and newest dancer; MIKA BARISTOKOVICK, ballet company leader.

TIME: Today.

SETTING: Empty stage with a mirror to practice dance steps in. A record player is Stage Right.

AT RISE: SUSAN enters. She is sad and alone in her leotards. She puts down her gear bag. She tries to do a few dance steps but can't get them just right. She does a few silly steps to break the glum mood.

SUSAN: *(Stops and sits alone in Center Stage; she buries her head in her hands for a few seconds as if she wants to cry but can't, then looks up at the audience. To herself:)* **It's happening. I'm getting too old to dance.** *(She gets up.)* **I just can't hit those high notes of ballet anymore.** *(Tries a few steps.)* **I can still do all the steps in my head, but my body, my legs, they just don't do it anymore for me.** *(She tries to tap dance while looking in mirror.)* **Well, I can always be a tap dancer. Do a buck and wing. But when it comes to ballet . . .** *(Tries a few jumps.)* **See? No spontaneity. Too slow. The zip is gone. I knew this would happen one day. But still, when it finally begins to happen, you find it hard to accept. But I will. I refuse to dance if I cannot give my audience perfection.** *(She sits defeated and alone in Center Stage.)* **Too old to dance. Me.** *(TAMI, MARLI, and BARBARA enter in leotards. They put down their gear bags and MARLI puts arm of record player on record. They begin to dance to music.)*

BARBARA: *(As she, MARLI, and TAMI dance)* **Hi, Susan. Are you resting again?** *(A little snide smile)*

SUSAN: **Do you mind?**

BARBARA: **No. Why would I mind?**

SUSAN: You're young. What do you know about anything anyway?

TAMI: You're right, Susan. All Barbara knows is ballet. She doesn't know one joke or one funny story.

MARLI: Unlike you, Sue. She has no sense of humor.

TAMI: Right.

MARLI: All Barbara does is dance.

BARBARA: I just live to dance.

TAMI: That's what we mean. Unlike Sue, all you ever think of is ballet.

MARLI: That and herself.

BARBARA: Dance is my life.

MARLI: Mine too.

SUSAN: Yes. Dance is my life too. But one has to laugh once in a while. *(Does a little tap dance.)* You have to do a little buck and wing once in a while, Barb.

TAMI: I agree.

MARLI: Right. Ballet is so serious.

BARBARA: Well, I'm sorry, but all I ever wanted to do was dance. That's how I've been since I was a little girl.

SUSAN: Me too. *(She tries to emulate the others but can't quite get it as good as she'd like, so she stops.)* But then one day you get old and the coordination begins to go. The muscles just begin to ache and the arms and legs just won't do what the brain tells them to. *(She sits Stage Front, far from others.)* And all of a sudden you realize ... it's over. It's all over. That great dream you had as a young girl to one day be the world's greatest ballerina will never be. Never.

MARLI: *(Stops dancing and walks over to SUSAN.)* Sue, are you all right?

SUSAN: Just a little sad. It's not easy to give up a dream.

MARLI: But you can't just give it up.

TAMI: *(Stops dancing and comes over to MARLI and SUSAN.)* Right. You can still dance. You're still part of the company.

SUSAN: I used to be the prima ballerina. *(Does following dances sitting down.)* Now . . . it's the hustle and a little buck and wing. I used to be the best, you know? Now —

BARBARA: I am! I'm the best. *(She shows off her best steps.)* I can do anything! The audience loves me. They think I'm everything beautiful, wonderful! When I dance, hearts beat just a little faster. I'm amazing.

MARLI: Will you listen to her?!

TAMI: I may throw up.

BARBARA: You all know it's true. I may be the newest dancer in the company, even the youngest — but I'm the best.

SUSAN: Yes, you are Barbara. You have all the energy and all the sparkle I had when I was your age.

BARBARA: And now you're old. *(The music stops, but BARBARA still shows off her technique, looking admiringly at herself in the mirror.)*

TAMI: Barbara, that's not very nice.

MARLI: Barbara is not a very nice person.

BARBARA: You can't be in this business. It's dog eat dog. If you don't look perfect, dance with absolute perfection, and smile a lot, you're out on your cute little ballerina butt. Like you, Sue. Know what I mean?

TAMI: Don't listen to her, Sue. You're still a good dancer. Right, Marli?

MARLI: Sure. Don't listen to Barbara.

BARBARA: Right, Sue. Don't listen to me. Listen to your legs. Are they telling you something?

TAMI: Barbara. Stop it!

SUSAN: No, Barbara is right. I'm getting too old to dance.

MARLI: No, you're not.

SUSAN: Yes, I am! *(TAMI and MARLI take a step back, SUSAN gets up and paces.)* I'm sorry for yelling. But what I don't want is pity. When it's over, it's over. I'll go quietly, Barbara. You can have center stage all to yourself. I won't get in your way.

BARBARA: When have you ever?

TAMI: You can be really mean, you know, Barbara?

BARBARA: I'm just being honest. *(SUSAN sits Downstage opposite of where she was before.)* **We all know that from the day I started with the company, I've been the apple of Mr. Baristokovick's eye. Of Mika's eye. He loves me.**

MARLI: Yeah, we've noticed, Barbara.

TAMI: One wonders how many bites Mr. B has taken out of a certain little rotten apple.

BARBARA: What are you insinuating?

SUSAN: Come on, girls. No fighting. OK? This is a ballet company. We're supposed to all be in sync. In harmony.

BARBARA: Now that is funny. Now that is a joke.

MARLI: You're the joke, Barbara. You think you're this beautiful, graceful sugarplumb fairy on your cute little toes. But we all know what you really are.

BARBARA: Oh, yeah. Then tell me. What am I?

TAMI: An ambitious little brat.

MARLI: With no heart.

BARBARA: Yep. That's me. And just look where it has gotten me.

SUSAN: Where has it gotten you, Barbara?

BARBARA: Right to the top of the ballet world. Here we are in New York, in the Big Apple. Everyone loves me. The critics love me. Did you see that article about me in the *New York Times?* And the one in *People?*

MARLI: Yeah, we saw them. Unfortunately, they left a few things out. I'm sure it was not intentional on their part.

TAMI: Right. Some people just have good press agents.

BARBARA: Yeah. Bernie's the best. Wasn't he your press agent once, Susan?

SUSAN: Yes, Barbara. You know he was.

BARBARA: Right. Back in the good old days, when you were younger.

SUSAN: **Right again.** *(She gets up as if to leave.)* **So it's all yours,**

Barbara. You can have the critics, center stage, and even Mika.

TAMI: No.

MARLI: Not Mr. B.

BARBARA: Yes. *(To SUSAN)* Oh . . . right. I forgot. He was yours once too, wasn't he?

SUSAN: He wasn't mine, as you put it. We were in love.

BARBARA: Like he and I are now.

MARLI: I really doubt that.

BARBARA: Oh, you do. Well, he's picking me up tonight. And we're flying off together for a few weeks in Europe.

SUSAN: You are?

BARBARA: We are. Are you surprised?

SUSAN: No. Not really. Mika always loved a pretty face.

BARBARA: Thank you.

SUSAN: Even if there's nothing but cotton candy behind it. *(MARLI and TAMI laugh.)*

BARBARA: Very funny. Ha, ha. You'll see. You'll all be surprised.

SUSAN: No, we won't.

BARBARA: No. I guess you won't be. *(SUSAN smiles.)* You seem to be taking this all so well, Susan, for an old person — one too old to dance, I mean. No offense. *(Sarcastic little smile)*

TAMI: You're so cruel, Barbara.

MARLI: I agree. You may be a great dancer, but you have no heart.

SUSAN: And you know, Barbara, you need more than your youth and good looks to stay on top. You need heart. And I really think that that is your weak point. Right, Tami?

TAMI: Right, Barbara. So be careful. You may yet end up out on your cute little ballerina butt.

BARBARA: I don't think so. Mika loves me. He thinks I'm wonderful. We're going to Europe for a wonderful vacation. This is like a fairy tale. Like a dream. What more can I ask for?

SUSAN: A big dose of reality.

TAMI: Right.

BARBARA: Who needs reality when I have such a lovely dream?

MARLI: You do.

SUSAN: And it will come. It always does. Life is like that. One lives and one learns.

BARBARA: I prefer to live and love.

SUSAN: I know. But you're young. You'll learn.

MARLI: Right.

TAMI: We all do.

SUSAN: In time.

BARBARA: In time I will be the greatest ballerina in the world. And what will you be, Susan, eh? What will you be?

TAMI: Susan will be ... *(Pauses to think.)*

MARLI: She'll be ... *(Pause)*

BARBARA: Yes? What will she be?

SUSAN: What will I be? I'll be the best ex-dancer in the Big Apple. *(Does a little tap step.)* **The best tap dancer in the world!**

TAMI and MARLI: And a great teacher!

MARLI: Yes!

TAMI: Right!

BARBARA: Oh, yeah? Who says?

MIKA: *(Enters, carrying sheet music.)* I say!

BARBARA: *(Running into his arms)* Mika! Already! You're early!

MIKA: *(Coldly)* Yes, I am. And I have been here for a while.

BARBARA: *(A bit afraid, backs away from him.)* You have?

MIKA: Yes. I forgot my music, so I came back to get it. And I was very surprised by what I heard.

BARBARA: You ... were? Just what did you hear?

MIKA: I heard a very conceited, unfeeling dancer.

BARBARA: Yes! Susan!

MIKA: No, Barbara. Not Susan. Susan was never conceited or unfeeling. Susan always had time for everyone. And

– 180 –

when Susan danced, every step came from here. *(Covers his heart.)* **From her heart.**

TAMI and MARLI: Yes.

MIKA: *(Puts his arm around SUSAN.)* **This one has enough heart for all the dancers in my company, even you, Barbara.**

BARBARA: Mika. What are you doing? I thought you loved me. Why are you holding her like that?

MIKA: Because I finally can see what is really important in life.

BARBARA: In life? What about us? What about dance?

MIKA: I was wrong about us.

BARBARA: Wrong? Mika. I love you. I thought you loved me.

MIKA: No. I guess I was in love with your beauty, even your technique. You are a wonderful dancer, Barbara — as far as technique is concerned. You have great potential. And I must confess, I do have a tendency to fall in love with beautiful, young dancers with great potential. But as one gets older, one lives and one learns.

SUSAN: Seems I've heard that one before.

MARLI: Yes, it does have a familiar ring to it. Right, Tami?

TAMI: Yes, right, Marli. But a nice ring.

BARBARA: Not to me.

MIKA: I can see that now. And that is why I'm making Susan my new assistant choreographer. *(TAMI, MARLI and SUSAN smile and act happy as BARBARA frowns.)*

BARBARA: But, Mika, you promised that to me!

MIKA: Yes. But that was before I realized you lacked one important quality.

BARBARA: What? What do I lack? I have youth, beauty, grace, technique. What could I possibly lack?

MIKA: Heart. You need a little help there.

TAMI and MARLI: More than a little.

MIKA: Yes. And that is going to be Susan's job. She is going to show you all you need to know about heart. Right, Susan?

SUSAN: You still want me?

MIKA: Yes. And I never want to lose you. Will you teach Barbara and the other dancers what you know about heart?

SUSAN: Yes. I'll do my best.

MIKA: You always do. So, Barbara, you must listen to Susan. Let her teach you what it means to have heart. She will start in three weeks.

BARBARA: *(Smiling)* After we get back from Europe, Mika?

MIKA: No. *(To SUSAN)* After Susan and I get back from Europe. You will come with me, Susan, won't you?

SUSAN: Why, Mika?

MIKA: Why?

SUSAN: Yes. Why?

MIKA: Two reasons.

MARLI: Two reasons?

TAMI: What are they?

BARBARA: Yeah. This I've got to hear.

SUSAN: Me too. I'd like to know both of your reasons, Mika.

MIKA: Well, reason number one is I'm in love with you, Susan. I know now I really am.

SUSAN: Ah-ha. I see. And what's the other reason?

MIKA: I think I need a little help in the heart department as well. I have a tendency to be heartless at times.

TAMI and MARLI: We've noticed.

SUSAN: Girls.

MIKA: No. They're right. So, Susan, will you come away with me? *(As he hugs her gently)* Will you teach me how to have a little heart?

SUSAN: Yes. *(MIKA and SUSAN embrace.)*

MIKA: *(He kisses her on forehead, then)* You've got a lot of heart, Susan. And that's why I love you — and will always love you. *(To others)* Now on with the dance! *(SUSAN and MIKA kiss and exit as curtain falls. BARBARA sits alone, MARLI puts on music and MARLI and TAMI dance to music.)*

SERIOUS DRAMA

The Runaway

PRODUCTION NOTES

PLAYERS: 2 women.

PLAYING TIME: 15 minutes.

SETTING: A park bench, trees behind bench, city skyline in background.

COSTUMES: MADGE in tattered coat, pants, wool hat, scarf, old boots, gloves, disheveled grey wig. JENNY in neat jeans and parka.

PROPERTIES: Shopping cart with shopping bags, old clothes, newspapers, toothbrush, insect spray, comb, toilet paper, teacup, teddy bear, galoshes, photo album.

LIGHTING EFFECTS: Fall night. Moonlight.

The Runaway

CHARACTERS: MADGE, a bag lady; JENNY, a runaway.

Scene 1

TIME: Fall, just before winter.

SETTING: A park bench, trees behind bench, city skyline in background. Moonlight.

AT RISE: MADGE enters. She pushes a shopping cart that contains shopping bags and all her possessions.

MADGE: *(Talking to herself as she pushes her cart back and forth, back and forth across stage)* **I don't know. I don't know. First they take away my room, then they tear down my little house — OK, OK, so what if it was a cardboard house? It was from good cardboard. A big box. But they tore it down, then they chase me out of the subway, out of the bus terminal, and out of the train station. Where do I go now? The Ritz? The Waldorf? Where do I sleep? They steal my money. They scare me away and say, "Get lost, you old goat!" Is that a nice way to treat an old woman? I ask you. Is it? That's for me to know and for you to find out. Whatever happened to respect for your elders? Take care of them. Treat them like human beings, like a person. I am a person, you know.** *(Bangs her chest with her fist.)* **I have feelings. Dignity! The doctors said I was sick. In the head. Me? Ha. I was never sick a day in my life. I was a mother! I had ...** *(Thinks, then)* **three, four kids. Where are they now?** *(Stops to think, then continues to pace.)* **They all forgot about me. The children, the city, the people. They try to act like we're invisible. We have no homeless, no bag people, no bums. Well, I'm not a bum. I'm a person. I've got feelings. I'm not invisible. I'm right here.** *(To skyline)* **See?** *(To audience)* **See? I'm a real person. I'm alive.**

I wasn't homeless all my life. No. I had a home once. A nice home. *(Thinks, then)* It was somewhere. I was someone. Then I got sick. I told them I wasn't sick. "I am not sick," I told them. No, I was not sick. I was fine. Just let me alone, leave me be. Go away, I told them. *(She walks over to bench and sits, takes a few breaths; she's puffing.)* Just let me rest. I'll be fine in a moment. And so here I am. I guess they let me out. They finally realized I was fine. So here we are. *(Looks around.)* Where are we? Looks like the park again. I don't like the park. I can't sleep here. Keep one eye open at all times, Madge, old girl. They want to take everything else you have. And don't put up a fight. Don't struggle. Just give in to their demands. You're old. They are young. They are strong. You aren't. So let them have it all, everything. Or they might hurt you. And what will you have then? *(Thinks)* My dignity? *(Shrugs)* Or did I lose that long ago with my pride, my home, my family, my children? And here I am.

Still . . . I am my own boss. No one tells Madge what to do, where to go, where to sleep. I have my independence. I am an independent woman. Yes, yes. I have that. No one is going to take away my independence. *(Pulls cart closer, protecting it.)* Or my bags. And don't tell me to go to those shelters. I prefer the park. It may not be as warm at night, but it's a lot safer here. That's what I say. Oh, they tell me different. But they lie. They all lie. You have to be careful. They're all liars today. Don't trust a soul. *(Just then, JENNY runs Onstage. MADGE sees JENNY and quickly grabs her cart, protecing it. JENNY looks around, trying to hide from someone.)*

JENNY: *(Afraid, puffing, she sits on bench beside MADGE, who moves away carefully.)* You see anyone after me?

MADGE: *(Scared)* No. I didn't see anyone.

JENNY: Good, because I ran away from home yesterday and I think the cops are after me.

MADGE: You ran away? From home?

JENNY: Yeah.

MADGE: Me too.

JENNY: When?

MADGE: *(Thinks, then)* **Not yesterday. Long ago ... I think. I forget just when. Why did you run away?**

JENNY: **I'm tired of everyone telling me what to do.**

MADGE: **I know what you mean.**

JENNY: **You do?**

MADGE: **Sure. You want to be your own boss. Be independent. Have no one telling you to do this, do that. Wear this, wear that.**

JENNY: **Right. How did you guess?**

MADGE: **You remind me of me.**

JENNY: *(Not happy about that)* **I do?**

MADGE: **You do. I hate people telling me where to go, what to do, when to get up, when to dress, what to wear. Now I do what I want when I want and I wear what I want when I want.** *(Shows her her clothes.)* **See? I found this myself. But I'm not sure where. Like it?**

JENNY: *(Appalled)* **It's ... OK, I guess.**

MADGE: **It's perfect.** *(Looks down at her garment.)* **Not one flea.** *(Picks a flea off.)* **Well, maybe one. But no ticks or lice. Nope. It's a good fabric. Did I tell you the best garbage was on Fifth Avenue? Or was it Fifty-seventh Street? Excellent garbage.**

JENNY: **Garbage?**

MADGE: **Yes. Excellent selection. Very fashionable, so long as you're thirty or forty years behind the times. Very few holes or fleas.** *(Sees a big hole in coat.)* **Well, maybe one.**

JENNY: **You got that coat out of the garbage?**

MADGE: **No, I bought it at Bloomingdales.** *(Points to blouse.)* **And this at Macys.** *(Points at pants.)* **And this at Gimbels.**

JENNY: **Gimbels went out of business years ago.**

MADGE: **Really?**

JENNY: Yes. Really.

MADGE: Well, I think I got these pants there. *(Thinks)* **Or maybe I got them at the Salvation Army. Maybe they were a gift? I don't know. I don't recall. So you been on the street long?**

JENNY: Just this morning. I was at a friend's house last night.

MADGE: You have a friend?

JENNY: Yes. Don't you?

MADGE: *(Shakes her head no.)* **No. You can't afford them on the street. Trust no one is my motto.**

JENNY: Do you trust me?

MADGE: About as far as I can throw you.

JENNY: That's not very nice.

MADGE: Nice? Nice is for family and friends. Out here on the street, you have to be careful. So you settle for cold, aloof, distant.

JENNY: Can't we be friends?

MADGE: *(Backing away a bit)* **Why?**

JENNY: Everyone needs a friend.

MADGE: No, thank you. I had one once and he beat me up.

JENNY: You don't think I would beat you up, do you?

MADGE: *(Backing away a bit more)* **You might. You look strong enough yet. You're new.**

JENNY: New?

MADGE: On the street. You're still strong. But after you get pneumonia a few times, bit by a rat or two, mugged, or worse, you won't be so strong. Then you'll be smarter. You won't be so nosey.

JENNY: I just want to be your friend. That's all. I don't want to rip you off, beat you up. Really. Don't you believe me?

MADGE: Why should I? I don't know you. Who are you?

JENNY: My name is Jenny. *(Puts her hand out to shake.)*

MADGE: *(Moves away more.)* **So?**

JENNY: What's your name?

MADGE: That's for me to know and you to find out.

JENNY: That's not very friendly. I just want to be your friend.

MADGE: Why?

JENNY: I told you. Everyone needs a friend.

MADGE: Well . . . I don't. I just want to be left alone. I like my freedom. I like my independence. *(Looks at JENNY, who smiles at MADGE and puts her hand out.)* I like being alone. *(Quickly shakes JENNY's hand.)* My name is Madge.

JENNY: Hi, Madge. Happy to meet you.

MADGE: Yeah? Why?

JENNY: *(Shrugs)* I guess because you're the first one I've talked to all day.

MADGE: Oh. Me too.

JENNY: I'm the first one you talked to all day?

MADGE: All month.

JENNY: Madge, aren't you lonely?

MADGE: *(Looks away from JENNY.)* Why should I be lonely?

JENNY: I don't know. I haven't talked to anyone for only a few hours and I'm lonely already.

MADGE: You'll get over that. Soon you'll forget all your old friends and they'll forget you. Your mother and father will forget you, you'll forget them. Do you have a boy friend?

JENNY: I did.

MADGE: They're the first to forget. Men. Here today, gone tomorrow.

JENNY: Yeah. I hate my life.

MADGE: I hate my life. No. Wait. I hate your life. Yes. My life I like. It's you who hates my life. Or do you like it? So, Jenny, do you like this life on the street?

JENNY: It's certainly free.

MADGE: Yep. Just stay out of the way of the police, the muggers, the crazies, the bums, the wild dogs —

JENNY: Wild dogs?

MADGE: Yeah. And rats. Rabies. Don't feed them. Hit them with a stick! Hard. It's them or us.

JENNY: I guess.

MADGE: You guess? Girl, it's fact. Facts of life on the street. Here, you're not careful, and you're suddenly living in Potter's Field, only you aren't living. So why you run away — besides the usual bad parents thing?

JENNY: That's it.

MADGE: Were they mean to you? Abusive?

JENNY: My parents?

MADGE: No, mine. Yes, your parents.

JENNY: No. They were just ... parents.

MADGE: Did you have a color TV?

JENNY: Yeah. So? Possessions aren't everything.

MADGE: True. But I was just wondering if Blase Lantana on that soap, The Edge of Death, is as cute as they say.

JENNY: He is.

MADGE: I knew it.

JENNY: Don't you ever see TV?

MADGE: Occasionally in store windows. But lately they chase me away before I get a chance to see the soaps.

JENNY: Oh.

MADGE: You'll see. Now they'll all love you. You look like money to them. A yuppie puppy I think they call it. You say to them: here's someone who'll be buying a color TV, a VCR, a CD player, a walkman. Me? When they see me, they see an eyesore — strange, unattractive odors — no sale. I upset them. Unnerve them. Give it time. Soon they'll want to throw you out too. You like sleeping in the park?

JENNY: I don't know. Is it safe?

MADGE: No. There's the mosquitoes, the rats, the gangs, the police. I keep one eye open at all times.

JENNY: Don't you have a home?

MADGE: Oh, yes. A condo on Park Avenue and a winter place

in Miami. No. *(Points to bench.)* **This is my home.**

JENNY: **This bench?**

MADGE: **The whole thing** — *(Looking at JENNY sitting on bench)* **or part of it anyway.** *(JENNY gets up.)*

JENNY: **Sorry, I didn't realize it was yours.**

MADGE: **Sit. Sit!** *(JENNY sits.)* **My house is your house.**

JENNY: **Thanks, Madge.**

MADGE: *(Backs away a bit.)* **How'd you know my name?**

JENNY: **You told me.**

MADGE: **I did?**

JENNY: **You did.**

MADGE: **Funny. I don't usually do that.**

JENNY: **So you don't have a home and you don't have a family, Madge?**

MADGE: **I did once. Long time ago.** *(Goes to get photo album out of her cart.)* **My photo album.** *(It contains her life's history and family photos before she hit the street. MADGE looks for it.)*

JENNY: **You carry your family album with you?**

MADGE: **Sure. I carry all the essentials, all the important things.** *(Holds each item up.)* **My toothbrush, my insect spray, my galoshes, my toilet paper, a comb, my teacup,** *(Holds up a teddy bear)* **my baby's teddy. I think it was my baby's. It was someone's baby's. And my photo album.** *(Sits close to JENNY.)* **Want to see?**

JENNY: **OK.**

MADGE: **It's old, but it's mine.**

JENNY: **Who's that? She's really pretty. Is she a model? Is that your daughter?**

MADGE: **That's me.**

JENNY: **It is?**

MADGE: **Yes. I told you it was a long time ago.** *(Looks at picture, thinks, smiles.)* **All the boys were crazy about me at school.**

JENNY: *(Points to another picture.)* **Who's this hunk? He's cute.**

MADGE: *(Turning page very coldly)* **My father. You wouldn't like him.**

JENNY: Why not?

MADGE: That's for me to know and you to find out. *(Turns page.)*

JENNY: *(Looking at picture)* Nice house. Yours?

MADGE: Yes. I loved that house. You were never cold in that house. There were no rats to bite you. No dirt or mess. Mama was very neat.

JENNY: Who's this woman with the baby?

MADGE: My mother. She died when I was two. That's me in her arms. *(Kisses picture and turns page.)* Look. See this guy?

JENNY: The chubby guy?

MADGE: *(Big smile)* Yeah. Uncle Sal. I wanted to go live with him and Aunt Jo.

JENNY: You didn't want to live with your father?

MADGE: That's for me to know and for you to find out.

JENNY: *(Looking at picture)* Is that you on your father's lap?

MADGE: *(Turning page quickly)* That's —

MADGE and JENNY: *(Together)* For me to know and for you to find out.

JENNY: I don't think you liked your father very much. *(MADGE is silent.)* So you wanted to run away and live with your Uncle Sal.

MADGE: And Aunt Jo. They always loved me. They had such beautiful Christmas trees. Uncle Sal would play Santa. *(Points to photo.)* See? Didn't even need a pillow for his belly. He'd decorate the house with a million lights.

JENNY: And your father didn't?

MADGE: No. I said I'd decorate, but he said no. And no was no. He didn't like Uncle Sal or Aunt Jo, but he ate their food. And borrowed money for beer and cigarettes. But he hated them. I loved them.

JENNY: Where are they now?

MADGE: *(Closes album)* Dead. Everyone's dead. *(Puts album away.)* It's just me and the rats now. You're a lucky kid. Your family is still alive. And they don't hurt you. Lucky.

JENNY: Sure, sure. Give me a break. All day it's Jenny do this, Jenny do that; Jenny, don't go out with this boy; Jenny, don't go out with that boy. Pick up your clothes, clean your room, lower the stereo. They never stop!

MADGE: When they stop, then you should run away. My father never had two words for me. *(Mumbles)* He did other things ... but never talked to me. He never really loved me. Your parents love you?

JENNY: *(Thinks, then shrugs.)* I guess. They just want me to do all the things I hate.

MADGE: Like clean your room?

JENNY: Yeah.

MADGE: Do they beat you?

JENNY: *(Shocked)* No. Never.

MADGE: You're lucky. Do they talk to you?

JENNY: God, all the time. They never stop.

MADGE: How's Christmas at your house?

JENNY: Daddy always brings home a big tree.

MADGE: Is he a good man?

JENNY: Both of my parents are OK. They just don't understand me. I don't understand me.

MADGE: They don't understand you? And you don't understand you. I don't understand you. They love you, you have a nice home, a big Christmas tree, a stereo, occasionally a *loud* stereo, and you want to live in the park on this bench with me?

JENNY: I don't know what I want.

MADGE: Ah, that's different. You're a normal teenager. What normal teenager knows what he or she wants?

JENNY: I'm so confused.

MADGE: It's your job to be confused. Accept it, kiddo. When you're old like me you can be unconfused. You can be smart. You can choose to abandon your life of opulence for the good life of meager rations, hungry rats, and this bench. Hey, go home, kid. Have some milk and cookies.

(Taps seat of bench.) **I'll keep your place warm for you. It'll always be right here. In ten, fifteen years when Prince Charming does you wrong, or you don't become a woman on Wall Street Week, you can come back, live in the park, and we can go over** *your* **family album. Be sure to bring your family album.** *(Mumbles to herself.)* **Because some day it will be all that's left.**

JENNY: I think I want to go home.

MADGE: Wait.

JENNY: Wait?

MADGE: Yes. Will you visit me?

JENNY: Here?

MADGE: Where else? The Waldorf? So will you? Visit me?

JENNY: Sure. *(JENNY gets up to go.)* Well . . . bye.

MADGE: Yeah. Right. Bye, kid.

JENNY: My name's Jenny, Madge.

MADGE: Sure. Right. Memory's a little fuzzy these days. It's all that ozone in the air if you ask me.

JENNY: I guess. *(JENNY is sorry to leave MADGE.)* Bye, Madge.

MADGE: Bye, already. Geez. Go.

JENNY: You going to be OK?

MADGE: I have my Raid and my Mace. What more do I need?

JENNY: I'll be back. I'll bring you some food or something.

MADGE: Sure, kid.

JENNY: Jenny.

MADGE: Bye.

JENNY: Bye. You sure you're going to be all right?

MADGE: Yeah. Get home. *(JENNY waves and exits.)* **I thought she'd never leave.** *(She spreads out newspapers on bench, sprays some insect spray around and on her.)* **Am I all right?** *(A little laugh, she lies on bench.)* **That's for me to know and for you to find out.** *(She covers her head with newspaper and goes to sleep as curtain falls.)*

The Family Barbecue

PRODUCTION NOTES

PLAYERS: 3 males; 2 females.

PLAYING TIME: About 25 minutes.

COSTUMES: Casual summer clothes, jeans, shorts, sneakers.

PROPERTIES: Hot dogs, hamburgers, salad, soda, picnic plates and forks, napkins, plastic cups, football.

The Family Barbecue

CHARACTERS: DANNY, a college student; GINA, Danny's older sister; JACK, Gina's husband; TOM, Danny and Gina's brother; SUE, Tom's wife.

TIME: Saturday afternoon.

SETTING: Backyard of JACK and GINA's house. Rear of house is on painted backdrop. There are trees in background, a barbecue Upstage Left and a picnic table Upstage Right. Table is set with salad, soda, plates. Some children's yard toys are in sight near rear of stage.

AT RISE: GINA, DANNY, TOM, and SUE are fixing hot dogs and hamburgers as JACK covers the extinguished barbecue after cooking.

SUE: So here we are.

JACK: A great day for a barbecue.

DANNY: Not bad. *(Takes a bite out of hamburger.)*

GINA: *(Looking up)* They said it was going to rain. But look at that sun. *(She eats some of her salad.)*

TOM: When are those weather reports ever right? When they predict a blizzard, we have a few flurries.

DANNY: And when they predict a few flurries, we end up with three feet of snow.

SUE: Yeah. Like last winter. But today it's beautiful. I love the summer. Makes you want to do so much. *(She drinks a cup of soda.)* Makes me feel romantic. Right, Tom? *(Puts her arm around TOM who munches on his hot dog.)*

TOM: *(Pretending not to be interested in SUE's affection)* Sure, sure. Later, Sue. *(TOM smiles to tease SUE.)* These hot dogs are great, eh? *(SUE pretends to slug him and TOM ducks.)* You can really cook 'em, Jack.

JACK: Thanks, Tom. Glad you like 'em. The key is to keep 'em hot, cook them evenly all over, all around. You have to keep turning them. You don't want to let them just sit there in one position and burn.

SUE: Right, Tom. Listen to Jack. He knows what he's talking about.

JACK: I do?

GINA: Jack's a great cook.

JACK: I sure am.

DANNY: Burgers are good, too.

JACK: My army training, I guess.

SUE: You were a cook in the army?

JACK: Yep.

GINA: College ROTC, you mean.

JACK: Right. We did a lot of camping. It was almost the army.

GINA: *(Teasing and flirting with him)* Almost isn't enough, Jack. Know what I mean?

JACK: *(Teasing her right back)* Women. Never satisfied.

GINA: Well ... almost never. *(Playfully changing the subject)* So, Danny, why didn't you bring Marnie? *(DANNY fixes himself a drink.)*

DANNY: She had to work today.

SUE: She going to stop by later?

DANNY: Yeah.

GINA: How's she doing?

DANNY: Great. She loves her job.

SUE: I want to work but Tom wants me to stay home with the kids.

GINA: But they're away at camp now. You can get a summer job, Sue. *(Puts her salad dish down on table and wipes her mouth with a napkin.)*

TOM: I don't want Sue to work.

SUE: See?

TOM: So how's your final semester at college going, Dan?

DANNY: Not bad. *(As they finish their food or drink, they put the cups or plates on table.)* It's hard to work and study. But in a few more months school will be over. Then Marnie and

I can get married.

GINA: Make it legal.

DANNY: Yeah. Then we can settle down like normal people.

GINA: Like Jack and me?

TOM: And Sue and me.

DANNY: Yeah. I guess. You are sort of . . . normal.

GINA: Thanks, Dan.

DANNY: It was just a joke, Gina.

JACK: What's the problem, Dan? Marriage too conservative for you?

DANNY: No. I think marriage is great, with the right person.

JACK: Like Marnie?

DANNY: Yeah.

SUE: So why do you seem so unsure?

DANNY: I guess things have been going so good as they are. You know? You hear all these stories about couples who were great together for years. Then they get married and — bam! They're getting divorced.

GINA: *(Stands close to JACK.)* We aren't.

DANNY: I know. You guys are great. You remind me of Mom and Dad.

GINA: *(Obviously upset, pulls away from JACK and walks away from DANNY.)* Oh, God. Please, Danny, don't start. *(Everyone seems to fall silent and move a bit apart.)*

DANNY: Sorry. But I just think we could have done more.

GINA: *(Turns to face him.)* Danny, we did all we could do, and you know it. There was nothing we could do.

SUE: There was nothing anyone could do. You heard what the doctors said. Right, Tom? *(TOM thinks.)* Tom?

TOM: Right. Sue's right, Danny.

GINA: Right. Listen to your brother. Right, Tom?

TOM: *(Not into this)* Yeah. Right.

DANNY: *(Looking at TOM)* You don't sound so sure.

GINA: Look, there's nothing we could have done for Dad or Mom that wasn't done. Right, Tom?

TOM: *(Now a bit more firmly)* **Right. Nothing.**

DANNY: That's what everyone says. Everything that could be done was done. Everyone seems so sure. I just wish I was as sure as everyone else. Even Marnie tells me to stop thinking about it.

JACK: She's right, Dan. She's a smart woman. Listen to her. We did all we could do, and so did the doctors.

GINA: Right. Regardless of how long they lingered in that hospital, Mom and Dad died, for all intents and purposes, in that car wreck.

SUE: Yes. It was just all those machines that were keeping them alive. Right, Tom?

TOM: Right, Dan. We did all we could. Everyone did.

DANNY: I know. But I still miss them.

JACK: Hey, I think we all do.

GINA: I still dream about them.

DANNY: Remember those touch football games we used to have with Mom and Dad at all their summer barbecues? Remember? When we were kids?

GINA: Yes. You, me and Tom.

SUE: Yeah, right. You played touch football?

GINA: Yes. Dad was always the captain.

JACK: Really.

SUE: Tom always talks about those good old days.

TOM: I do?

SUE: Yeah, but it's OK. I love when you tell me all those stories about growing up.

TOM: I can get redundant at times.

SUE: Redundant. Listen to him. The journalist in him coming out. All I can say, kiddo, I've known you now for twelve years; we've been married for ten, and I never get tired of hearing about you growing up and how you used to play touch football. Hey, these are the important things, you know.

TOM: I never thought they were very important.

DANNY: Yeah. You never realize what is and what isn't important until it's too late.

GINA: True. But come on, guys. This is a barbecue. We're supposed to be having a good time. You know?

DANNY: I just can't help remembering them, especially when we have these barbecues. Remember the ones we had at Mom and Dad's?

GINA: Yes, yes. Dan, let's change the subject. All right? They're gone. We have to let them go. We have to.

DANNY: It's hard to do that, especially when they died the way they did. For no reason. Crushed by a truck: a sixteen-wheeler, driven by some drunk! And he's free, and Mom and Dad are dead.

GINA: Here we go.

DANNY: It was murder.

TOM: It was an accident.

DANNY: How can you say that? He was drinking! The truck driver was drinking!

GINA: Danny. We've gone over this a million times.

DANNY: So? What are you saying?

JACK: *(To DANNY)* Easy, guy.

SUE: Come on, Dan.

TOM: It's history.

DANNY: History?

JACK: Come one, Dan. You know what we all mean.

DANNY: I know, I know. It just gets me so aggravated that that drunk is out walking the streets.

TOM: He just wasn't drunk enough.

DANNY: What is that supposed to mean? Not drunk enough. He was drunk enough to kill them.

GINA: Legally, he was not drunk. *(She shrugs.)* That's the law. It was an accident.

DANNY: Well, it's a stupid law. He should be in jail for murder.

TOM: Look, we're getting all upset again. Danny, stop. OK?

DANNY: I just don't want to forget them.

GINA: Now how can we forget them? Danny, they're our parents. We'll never forget them.

DANNY: You seem like you want to.

GINA: No I don't!

DANNY: *(Sarcastically)* Yeah, right.

JACK: Danny, come on. That's not fair.

GINA: Right! You think you're the only one who is hurting? My heart is breaking! Mom and Dad were very close to me. And Dad and I were always close. You know that. When we were kids, he used to call me *(She pauses unable to talk, then)* his little girl. Bounced me on his knee. You and Tom were his big boys. But I was his little girl. I know I'm the oldest. But you know Dad. A good heart, but a male chauvinist to the end. *(She tries to smile.)* When I was little, he used to build me doll houses, take me for pony rides. Mom taught me how to cook and drive. They both did everything for us. *(After a pause, to DANNY)* You think I like any of this? You think I like what happened to them? I hate it. It stinks! *(Nearly in tears)* I miss him. I miss her. I miss them!

TOM: *(Putting his hand on GINA's shoulder)* We all hate what happened. But here we are, like it or not. We have to go on living. For the kids. For us. You and Marnie are going to get married, have a family and go on. That's how life is. You know? You have to go on living.

DANNY: That's what they say.

SUE: It's true. My mother died when I was fifteen. She had cancer. I thought I'd never be able to go on. Like she died when I needed her the most. But you go on. You manage. The pain fades. The memories never do. But you go on. Now I have Tom and our kids. We're a family. We all are. So life goes on.

JACK: It sure does. *(Not knowing what else to say)* So . . . how about another hamburger, Dan?

DANNY: No thanks. *(After some silence)*

GINA: You know, we do still have to talk about their house.

DANNY: Oh, so that's it. You're worried about their money, their house.

TOM: Danny, you know that's not what Gina means.

DANNY: Oh, no? Then why don't you tell us what you mean, Gina?

GINA: I just mean that that is our house. It's all that Mom and Dad left us. And I don't want us to have to sell it. It's so full of memories.

JACK: Gina has a point there, Dan.

DANNY: I know. I hate having to sell their house.

SUE: Why don't you and Marnie live in it, Dan?

GINA: Yeah!

DANNY: *(A little laugh)* We can't afford it.

TOM: Look, it's just a house.

DANNY: Well, it was their house, our house. I hate to see someone else living in it. It just doesn't seem right. I hate this.

TOM: Hey, Dan, we all do.

GINA: Yeah.

JACK: Life is never fair.

DANNY: Well ... someone has to be to blame! Someone.

GINA: Danny, it just happened.

DANNY: Things like this just don't happen. Not to Mom and Dad. They can't just say no one is responsible! They can't. Someone has to be responsible!

TOM: They aren't. We are. We have to forget about this, Dan.

DANNY: I'll go to court. I'll sue the truck company.

GINA: *(Throws her hands up.)* Great. Now he's going to take the truckers to court.

DANNY: *(Pacing)* Right! I'll get them. You'll see. If I have to I will. It looks like I'm all Mom and Dad has left. Besides, it's not right to just sweep all this under the rug. We can't just forget this.

TOM: Forget this? Who's forgetting this?

SUE: I'm not.

JACK and GINA: Neither are we.

DANNY: All I know is when Marnie or I — or any of you — are driving down the street, or crossing the street, and some jerk who's been drinking plows into you, I would hope that the drunk would be held accountable for what he does to any of you, or me. Or what about you, Gina? That could have been you. Would you like us to be trying to forget about you? You think Mom and Dad would want us to forget about them?

GINA: You really get me angry, Daniel, you know? What makes you think Dad or Mom wants us to go on grieving forever. To live like this. We have to think of our kids. They need us. They need us strong. Strong for them. Strong for us. And you have to be strong for Marnie. And for you. You have your whole life to think of. You know what I'm saying, Danny? *(DANNY says nothing.)*

TOM: Gina's right, Dan. You know how Mom and Dad were. They were so active. They'd want us to be happy.

GINA: They never sat around moping. Mom and Dad jogged. They rode their bikes all over town.

SUE: I remember.

JACK: Same here.

TOM: Dad went hunting and fishing, camping with us.

GINA: He and Mom went skiing. They were both active. They wouldn't like to see us grieving or arguing over them.

SUE: Gina's right, Dan.

JACK: Yes. I agree.

DANNY: Look, I'm not arguing. I just don't want us to forget them.

TOM: *(Slaps him gently on the back.)* Hey, Danny, my brother, they were our parents. How can we forget them?

SUE: I'll never forget either of them, especially your mom, Danny. She was in ways like my own mom. My kids never knew my mother. Only yours. She was special to them

– 204 –

and to me. I won't forget her, ever. I sort of thought she and your dad would go on forever. They were so active. But these things just happen, I guess, like with my mom. People don't, you know, live forever.

JACK: Sue's right.

DANNY: Yeah? Well, I remember Dad saying he wanted to live forever. He used to grab us all after those touch football games, hug us and say how much he loved us.

TOM: And he did.

GINA: And so do we. This is not easy for any of us, Dan. Come on, Danny, You know that. It's terrible. But we have to go on with all our lives. When I see you like this, so sad, it breaks my heart. You were always the family comedian, the funny one. You used to make me laugh. Now ... Danny, you're not so funny anymore.

DANNY: *(After a long pause)* So what are you saying? Because it hurts you to see me like this, you want me to forget them?

JACK: No. That's not what Gina said.

DANNY: Well, whatever she said, maybe you can forget them, but I can't. You were always the cold one, Gina, you know?

SUE: *(Shocked)* Danny!

DANNY: It's true! She was always the cold one. No feelings!

GINA: *(Slaps him, then is sorry. He rubs his cheek.)* I'm sorry, Danny. I'm sorry.

DANNY: Sure, sure.

TOM: Danny, you know we all love Mom and Dad. And you know Gina does, too.

GINA: Right. Danny? I'm sorry I slapped you. But you make me so mad sometimes. You act like we don't care about Mom and Dad. That we'd just rather forget them and go on with our barbecues like nothing has happened. But you know why I wanted you all here?

DANNY: No. Why?

GINA: Because you're all I have left. You know? *(Her emotions slowly build.)* It's just you guys and me. And the kids. I need

you. *(Being more firm)* **And what I want is not all this morbid talk about death, but happy memories of Mom and Dad playing touch football with us, memories of Mom and Dad skiing, of us as a happy family.** *(More emotional)* **I don't want to remember them in the hospital, or at the funeral — or at the cemetery. OK? I want to remember them here at the barbecues with us!** *(She's in tears.)* **Can't you see that?!**

DANNY: *(Tries to reach out to her, half looks at her and half wanting perhaps to hug her, but there is a distance between them.)* **I'm sorry, Gina.**

TOM: *(Still a bit unsure)* **Dan, you know as well as we do that they're gone — but not forgotten.**

DANNY: **I know. But still sometimes I wonder. I mean it seems so wrong to just go about our lives . . .**

TOM: **You can't feel guilty about that. We did all we could. You, me and Gina have nothing to feel guilty about. Nothing.**

DANNY: **Can you say they are dead and it was just an unavoidable accident? Can you, Gina? Say it. Go ahead. I want to hear you say it. Say it.** *(GINA is silent and hurt and disappointed.)* **You can't even say it. Mom and Dad are dead and it was just some silly, unavoidable accident. Go ahead, Gina. If you're so sure, so trusting in all those cops and lawyers, and doctors, say it. Mom and Dad are dead and it was all just a silly, somewhat unfortunate, but totally unavoidable accident. Go ahead. Say it!**

SUE: **Come on, Dan. Stop this.**

JACK: **Yeah. I think you're being very unfair to your sister.**

DANNY: **Look, all I want to hear is Gina say it. Come on, Gina. Tell me. Mom and Dad are dead and it was all just one big unfortunate accident. Go ahead. Say it!**

GINA: *(She turns away.)* **I can't!**

DANNY: **See? She can't. What Gina wants is for *us* to say it. For me to say it.** *(To TOM)* **For you to say it. For us all to**

agree to say it. It was all just an accident. There is nothing we could have done. There is no one to get angry at. Things like this just happen. If we all agree on that, then she can feel it's OK to go on living happily ever after. *(GINA is obviously hurt by this.)*

TOM: Come on, Dan. That's not fair to Gina.

SUE: No. It's not.

JACK: I'll say. It's not fair, Dan!

TOM: *(To DANNY)* You're being unfair to her and to us.

DANNY: *(Looking at GINA and TOM)* I am? I am?

GINA: Yes, you are. I can't go on like this. I miss them! You know? I need you guys to help me. We have to share this thing. We have to try to be happy. I don't want this to destroy us. We were always so close. Danny, my kids love you. They think you're a great uncle. And you know I love you. You know I loved Mom and Dad. I still do. We all do. But we can't go on like this.

TOM: Gina's right, Dan.

DANNY: I just think it's so unfair. It's just not fair! We never did anything bad to anyone. Why did this have to happen to them? To us? *(He sits on picnic bench.)* It's not fair.

GINA: *(As she and TOM sit beside him, putting their hands on his back)* Bad things just happen sometimes. That's life. You know? It's just fate. The way things turn out.

SUE: Right. Like with my mom. Who knows why.

JACK: Right. No one knows why they happen, but they do.

GINA: This is real life. It's not something you see on Tv or read about in the newspapers. It's real. And it's happening to us. And we have to go on with our lives. Right, Tom? *(TOM thinks.)* Tom?

TOM: *(Gets up.)* Yes. When you see these things on TV, they seem so far away. You say, let them go. Let them rest in peace.

DANNY: But when it's your own parents, it's not like TV. *(They all are silent.)*

SUE and JACK: No.

GINA: So what are we going to do? We can't go on like this.
It's not fair to Mom and Dad. They wouldn't want us to
go on like this. We have to try to go on with our lives.
You and Marnie do, Sue and Tom do, and Jack and I do.
OK? Right, Tom? Help me. I thought you were on my side.

DANNY: On your side? Gina, this is not some political event.
Some contest. There are no sides here.

GINA: You know what I mean. Tom? Tell Danny. Tell your
brother what I mean. Tell him!

SUE: Come on, guys. No more fighting. OK?

JACK: Right. This is supposed to be a family barbecue.

TOM: So no more fighting.

GINA: Right, right, right. OK . . . I don't want to fight. So come
on, Danny. We need you. Tom? Am I right?

TOM: Yeah. We can't keep arguing over this. Gina's right,
Dan. You don't want all these summer barbecues — all
our family gatherings — to turn into fights over what
happened to Mom and Dad, do you?

DANNY: No.

GINA: *(Paces, then after a long pause)* **Then for God's sake, what
do you want?!**

DANNY: What do I want? I want Mom and Dad back!

GINA: *(Nearly in tears)* **Well, you can't have them back! They
are dead! Grow up, will you?! They died in that car wreck!
They are gone! Gone! And we have to bury them! Don't
you undertstand? Don't you get it?**

TOM: *(Sits alone)* **This is too much.**

SUE: Maybe we should go.

GINA: No!

TOM: We're staying.

GINA: Tell him, Tom. Tell Danny Mom and Dad are dead.

TOM: Gina. Please. He knows that.

GINA: No he doesn't! I need your help. Tell him. Tom?

TOM: Gina.

GINA: Jack!

JACK: Gina.

GINA: *(To DANNY)* We've gone on like this long enough. It has to stop! Now! Now! Now!

SUE: We better go.

GINA: No, no! Stay!

TOM: We're staying, we're staying.

DANNY: Maybe I should go.

GINA: No, don't! Danny, don't go! I need you, too!

DANNY: *(With a bit of sarcasm)* Really? You do, eh?

GINA: Yes, I do. You're my brother.

TOM: Maybe what we all need here is a little more time. Even you, Gina. *(As they all sit around table, TOM and DANNY each take one of GINA's hands, they sit a little closer and GINA squeezes their hands.)*

GINA: I'm sorry. *(After a pause)* I'm sorry I yelled. Maybe we do need a little more time.

DANNY: I know I sure do.

GINA: *(Squeezes their hands again.)* Yeah. OK. But we have to promise to try to cheer up, Dan. I hate seeing you so sad. You're supposed to be the funny one. What did Dad always call you?

DANNY: The joker.

TOM: I remember.

SUE: Me, too.

GINA: This has hurt all of us, maybe you the most, Dan, since you're the youngest. But you have to get over this. You have to try to smile a little, Danny. We all have to smile more, you know? We can't just mope about. Right? Tom?

TOM: Yeah.

GINA: Danny?

DANNY: I'll think about it.

GINA: That's all I ask. I need you guys. You are my brothers. *(Hugs them.)* Right? Family? *(To DANNY)* Danny?

DANNY: *(Nods)* Yeah. Of course. We're still a family.

GINA: Tommy?

TOM: Of course, Gina. We'll always be a family.

GINA: Yes. Always.

SUE: Ahh. *(SUE holds TOM's hand as JACK holds GINA's hand.)*

TOM: Gina, like I said, I think — no, I'm *sure* what we all need here is a little more time to sort this all out, without arguing.

DANNY: I agree. OK, Gina?

GINA: Yeah. And again I'm sorry if I yelled.

DANNY: Same here.

GINA: And I'm sorry I slapped you, Danny.

DANNY: *(Rubbing his cheek, a little smile at her)* Me, too. You've got some arm. Too much touch football.

GINA: *(Smiles at him, pets his cheek.)* I guess.

TOM: *(He gets up, pulls a football out from under table.)* Hey, look what I found.

DANNY: Geez.

TOM: Come on. Suddenly, I want to have a game of touch.

GINA: Me, too. Danny, Sue, Jack. You up for a game?

SUE: *(As JACK and SUE get up)* Sure.

JACK: Great idea.

DANNY: *(TOM tosses ball to DANNY, who stands holding it silently for a few seconds. Then smiles. They get ready to put the ball in play.)* Three, two, one — hike! *(They run about playing touch football as curtain falls.)*

The Funny Man

PRODUCTION NOTES

PLAYERS: 2 males; 1 female.

PLAYING TIME: About 8 minutes.

COSTUMES: BILLY in hospital gown; TERRY in pretty dress; TOM in sports jacket.

PROPERTIES: 2 envelopes, each with a letter in it.

LIGHTING EFFECTS: Spotlight that can follow actors and be dimmed.

The Funny Man

CHARACTERS: BILLY, a dying comedian; TERRY, his girl friend;
TOM, Billy's brother.

TIME: Now and then.

SETTING: A dark stage with hospital bed Upstage Center with
BILLY in it. He has intravenous lines in him.

AT RISE: A dark stage. Spotlight comes up on TOM, who stands
Downstage.

TOM: *(To audience)* **My brother died today. He was a funny
man.** *The* **funny man. That's what everyone called Billy.
Everyone knew Billy. But no one really knew him. All
they saw was the funny man who told these biting jokes
and silly stories. But now Billy's gone.** *(Pause)* **I'm going
to miss him. He was my brother.** *(Pause, then)* **If you would
have known him, you'd feel the loss I do. We all needed
Billy. We all need a good laugh now and then. But he's
gone.** *(Takes out an envelope.)* **Just before he died, however,
he gave me this. He told me not to open it until he was —
quote, "six feet under." He knew he was dying. Yeah. He
did. Cancer. He tried to fight it as long as he could.** *(Pause,
then)* **Anyway, he gave me this envelope. But before I open
it, let me tell you a little more about my brother Billy.
Actually, let me show you.** *(TOM puts envelope in his jacket
pocket as spotlight comes up on BILLY's bed with BILLY in it.)*
This was his hospital bed. And *thereees* **Billy! It's the day
before we lost him. His girl friend and I were just a couple
of the many visitors he had during those last few days.
He tried his best to keep everyone laughing. And we tried
our best to keep his spirits up, but it was no laughing
matter for any of us.** *(A little smile)* **I say that with tongue
in cheek.** *(A little smile of remembrance, pause, walks to other
side of stage.)* **Yeah. It seems Billy was doing all he could**

– 212 –

to keep our spirits up. *(TERRY enters.)* **Ah, enter the girl friend, Terry. She and Billy were really in love.** *(Lights dim out on TOM and spotlight comes up on BILLY and TERRY.)*

TERRY: *(Kisses him, then)* **So how you doing, Billy?**

BILLY: **Does miserable, terrible, lousy, ring a bell?**

TERRY: **You feel bad, eh?**

BILLY: **Only when I laugh.** *(He gives a little laugh.)* **Ooo, it hurts.**

TERRY: *(Holding his hand)* **I'm here, honey.**

BILLY: **Hear any good jokes lately?**

TERRY: **No. You?**

BILLY: **Yeah! Did you hear the one about the traveling salesman and the farmer's daughter?**

TERRY: **No. And I don't want to. It's sexist.**

BILLY: **Terry, I'm dying here. I can't just tell it this one last time?**

TERRY: **Nope. Know any others?**

BILLY: **I got a million of 'em, kiddo, but lately I'm not all that motivated. You want to hear sob stories, I got a few of those. Mr. Weinstein lost his leg yesterday. He said, "Doc, do you think I'll have a limp?" And Mrs. Costello had a hysterectomy. She said to the nurse, "So I guess my childbearing years are over." The lady is seventy-two years old!**

TERRY: **Gee.**

BILLY: **Gee is right. Jokes I used to hear. Now it's, "My head hurts, my leg hurts, I got a bump here, a lump there. Is this a tumor or am I just glad to see you, doc?"**

TERRY: *(She smiles.)* **You're so funny.**

BILLY: **Hey, you have to be in this terminal ward. Dying is no joke. I'm not laughing,** *(He coughs, and grows a little sad)* **you know, Ter.**

TERRY: *(Squeezes his hand.)* **I know. But I'm here.**

BILLY: **Yeah. You're all right, Terry. You were always my best critic. And my best friend. When you laughed, I knew**

– 213 –

I had a winner. Remember that joke I did on the President
of France?

TERRY: Oh, that one. Er . . . he didn't like it.

BILLY: Sure he did. He sent me a telegram.

TERRY: Telling you he was a bit annoyed.

BILLY: Annoyed-shamoid. He loved it!

TERRY: You told him you were dying.

BILLY: Yeah. I did. But I'm big in France, you know?

TERRY: We know.

BILLY: Yeah. They even gave me a medal for my comedies.
They love all my old movies over there. So when I said
to Monsieur President I am going to a far, far better place
than I have ever been . . . *(A little cough)*

TERRY: What did he say?

BILLY: He said, "Break a leg." Of course, he said it in French.
(He gives a little laugh.) He's all right.

TERRY: You're too much. *(Spotlight dims out and comes up on
TOM.)*

TOM: He was. My brother knew how to make everyone feel
good. He had this seemingly biting — even harsh — sense
of humor. You'd think when he made a joke about someone,
he hated their guts. But he didn't. Not Billy. Despite what
most of the world thought, Billy was a kind, gentle man.
He had a big heart. He helped out many charities and
never asked for anything, not even travel expenses. So
that last day, when I went to see him just prior to his
death, I had all I could do to laugh when he told a joke.
(TOM walks over to BILLY as spotlight follows TOM.) Hi, Billy,
Terry. *(To BILLY)* So what's new, bro?

BILLY: Did you hear the one about the traveling salesman
and the farmer's daughter?

TOM: Bill, not in front of Terry.

BILLY: Terry, go powder your nose. I want to tell my brother
that joke and he's afraid it might burn your ears off. So
it's off to the powder room for you.

TOM: No, no. Terry can stay. I don't want to hear that joke, Billy. OK?

BILLY: OK, OK. But you're both missing a big laugh.

TERRY: That's not what I heard.

BILLY: No? What did you hear?

TOM: We heard you tried to tell it to that cute little blonde nurse and she blushed so badly they had to let her go home.

BILLY: Talk about being red in the face, that girl sure was. But she was laughing.

TERRY: Yes. So much so they had to put a paper bag over her head.

BILLY: A paper bag?

TOM: She was hyperventilating.

BILLY: Oh, right. I figured they didn't do it because of her looks. That girl sure wasn't ugly. Now they should put a paper bag over Mrs. McGruter's head. That's an ugly nurse.

TERRY: You exaggerate.

BILLY: All I know is if Mrs. McGruter entered some heart attack patient's room on a dark night, she would blow out the heart monitor. *(No one laughs, pause, then)* **Laugh, already. I'm dying here.** *(They try to laugh.)* **Not a ten on the applause meter, eh? But, hey, for this place, I'll take what I can get from an audience.**

TOM: So how's the food in here, Billy?

BILLY: Food? What do I know about food? They feed me through a tube in my arm. Last night I had this really mouth-watering sugar water, just a snack before bedtime. This morning for breakfast, sugar water; for lunch, sugar water; for dinner, sugar water. I'm a happy man. Finally, I'm losing weight. You should try it yourself, Tom. A sugar water diet. It's very effective. Weight comes right off. Of course, it helps to have what I have to go with it.

TOM: Not very funny, Bill.

BILLY: Funny? You want to hear funny, I'll tell you that traveling salesman joke. There was this traveling salesman —

TOM: Billy, I don't want to hear that one. OK?

BILLY: OK. So how about you, Terry? We'll tell Tom to go powder his nose and I'll tell you the joke. OK?

TERRY: You don't want Tom to leave, do you?

BILLY: What can I do? He won't let me tell my joke, and I'm not going to be around here for a second show. This is it, kiddo. You hear the joke now, or it's curtains. So what do you say?

TERRY: Later. How are the nurses treating you?

BILLY: I'm very unhappy with them.

TOM: Aren't they giving you the help you need?

TERRY: Fluffing up your pillow?

TOM: Making you comfortable?

BILLY: Yeah.

TERRY: So . . . what's the problem?

BILLY: They cut my sponge baths down to one a day!

TERRY: Ahhh, can I give you one?

BILLY: With my little brother here?

TOM: I can go powder my nose.

BILLY: No, no. You stay. But when I'm gone, you can powder Terry's nose.

TOM: Hey, Bill, easy.

BILLY: She loves it. Right, Ter?

TERRY: You're a barrel of laughs.

BILLY: I'm one big joke, eh? Too bad I already know the punch line.

TOM: You're going to make it, Billy. You always do.

BILLY: No. I'm going to bomb out here. It's a bad house. Mrs. Goldberg, the night nurse, even said my traveling salesman joke was not funny. What? She thinks I'm unfunny. Hey, I'm the funny man. Right?

TOM and TERRY: Right.

BILLY: Right. *(Takes envelope out from under covers, very seriously)* Tommy, here. Take this. But promise me one thing.

TOM: *(Takes envelope)* Anything, Billy.

BILLY: Promise me you won't read it until I'm ... you know, working the biggest house of all *(Points to heaven)*, *the* palace, shall we say, in the sky. To put it bluntly, until I'm six feet under. OK?

TOM: *(Takes letter)* OK. I'll open it after ... you know.

BILLY: I know already, I know. *(He begins to cough horribly as TERRY hugs him and spotlight follows TOM to front of stage.)*

TOM: So Billy died. I buried my brother today. And now it's time to open this letter he entrusted to me before his death. *(TOM opens letter and is torn between tears and laughter.)* Let me read it to you: "There was this traveling salesman *(Lights dim out and curtain falls)* and this farmer's daughter ... *(Curtain)*

Barriers

PRODUCTION NOTES

PLAYERS: 2 women.

PLAYING TIME: About 15 minutes.

COSTUMES: BELLE is in old housecoat and slippers. SANDY in jeans, T-shirt, sneakers. A coat for SANDY.

PROPERTIES: Old wheelchair, new racing wheelchair, photo album.

LIGHTING EFFECTS: Lights can be dimmed out.

Barriers

CHARACTERS: BELLE, Sandy's mother; SANDY, a college woman in a wheelchair.

TIME: Today.

SETTING: The stage should suggest the barest essence of the living room of a comfortable old house. It is BELLE's house, the house where SANDY was born and raised. A small Venus de Milo sits on a lamp table. A photo album sits on a coffee table.

AT RISE: BELLE enters pushing an old, empty wheelchair.

BELLE: **This old chair.** *(Annoyed)* **Where can I put it now?**
(SANDY rolls in seated in new racing wheelchair.)

SANDY: **Mom, who are you talking to?** *(Looking around, picks up the small sculpture. Looks it over.)*

BELLE: **No one.**

SANDY: **No one? I heard you talking to someone.** *(Puts sculpture down on table.)*

BELLE: **No. I wasn't talking to anyone. I was just mumbling to myself.**

SANDY: *(Looking at old wheelchair)* **What are you doing with my old chair?** *(Looking it over)*

BELLE: **Pushing it out to the garage. I guess you won't be needing it now, since you bought that new one while you were away at college.**

SANDY: *(Racing around, doing a wheelie if possible)* **You're right about that, Mom. You're looking at the new Sandy.**

BELLE: *(Mumbling to herself)* **I think I liked the old one better.**

SANDY: *(Still riding around, not hearing BELLE)* **What, Mom? Did you say something?**

BELLE: **Oh, no, no. Nothing, baby. Just mumbling.**

SANDY: *(Rolls over to face her mother.)* **Mom, please don't call me that.**

BELLE: *(Acting as if she has no idea what SANDY means)* **Call** you what? I don't know what you mean.

SANDY: Mom, you know exactly what I mean.

BELLE: No. I don't. Really.

SANDY: Yes you do. I told you not to call me that anymore.

BELLE: Call you what, baby?

SANDY: *(A little louder, annoyed)* That.

BELLE: *(A little louder, imitating SANDY)* What?

SANDY: *(More frustrated than mad)* Baby!

BELLE: Oh. That.

SANDY: Yes, that. I hate it. I'm not a baby anymore. I hate it when people treat me as if I were. I'm a woman. I'm about to graduate from college. I am not a child. And you — my mother — above all people, should know that.

BELLE: I'm sorry, but college or no college, you'll always be my baby.

SANDY: *(Angry and frustrated)* But I'm not a baby anymore, Mom. *(SANDY moves farther away as she says each thing she now does.)* I'm about to graduate from college, I drive, I live away from home . . . *(Pauses, then turns and looks BELLE in the face.)* I have Tom, who loves me.

BELLE: *(Sarcastic)* Wonderful.

SANDY: That's right.

BELLE: *(Ironic)* Sure, sure.

SANDY: Mom, just because Dad walked out on you, and you hate men, don't think I do. I don't. I met a lot of great guys at school.

BELLE: *(Not happy)* Wonderful.

SANDY: Yeah. Right. They were.

BELLE: Oh? Tell me more. I think you owe me that much.

SANDY: Owe you? Is that how you see it?

BELLE: *(Cut off)* You owe me —

SANDY: Mom, I owe you a lot. I could never repay you for all you've done for me. But I have my own life now. My own needs.

BELLE: Needs? What needs do you have? Ramps? Curb cuts?

Elevators? You have all that.

SANDY: We don't have all that, and that's not what I mean. And you know it.

BELLE: I don't know what you mean. What could you possibly need?

SANDY: I need Tom. He needs me. We need each other.

BELLE: You don't need anyone.

SANDY: Everyone needs somone. You need someone.

BELLE: Who do I need? I have you.

SANDY: Mom, I'm away at college most of the year. And you're all alone.

BELLE: No, I'm not. I have the church, my bridge club. I enjoy endless nights of bingo. Have you ever been in a bingo parlor with six hundred men and women who love to smoke? *(Coughs)* It's wonderful. It's my life. I love it. Bingo and church. What more could I ask for?

SANDY: You haven't been to church since I left for college.

BELLE: So I have bingo. And besides the smoke, there's bagels and pastries. What more can any woman ask for?

SANDY: A lot more.

BELLE: OK. So I have my bridge club.

SANDY: Your bridge club broke up months ago.

BELLE: It did not. Who told you that?

SANDY: Mrs. Goldberg.

BELLE: *(Annoyed)* That one. I should have known. She's a senile old liar and a ... a gossip. She's got Alzheimers if you ask me, not to mention heart trouble, weak kidneys, osteoporosis, bad breath, rotten teeth, the gout, and fallen arches.

SANDY: No, she does not. She doesn't have any of those things, and especially not Alzheimers.

BELLE: What are you studying at that college? Medicine? Are you a doctor?

SANDY: No, I'm not a doctor.

BELLE: Then how can you be sure Goldberg isn't a basket case?

SANDY: Mom, she saw me down at the post office and gave me a big hello. "Hi, Sandy! How're you doing? How's your mom?" She asked me all about you. She said she misses you. She said she hasn't seen you in months.

BELLE: See? She forgot already. God, that woman has a memory like a sieve. *(Sarcastically, jokingly)* I saw her only last week when I took her to her Memory Expansion class at the Senior Citizen's Center. What? She forgot already?

SANDY: Mom, stop lying.

BELLE: Lying? Who's lying? The old lady just forgot. She does that all the time. She forgets she does it, but she does it.

SANDY: Mom, come on. Is something wrong? Are you all right?

BELLE: *(Sits in old wheelchair, sarcastically)* I'm fine. So how are you?

SANDY: Mom, you don't look fine. Does it have anything to do with the fact that I'm not coming home after college?

BELLE: No.

SANDY: You're not upset that I'm moving into an apartment of my own after graduation?

BELLE: *(Getting up and walking to edge of stage)* No.

SANDY: I think you are. *(Wheels over to her mother.)* Mom, you just can't accept the fact that I'm going to be out on my own.

BELLE: That's ridiculous. Stop it.

SANDY: Stop what? Stop telling you I'm not you're little baby anymore? Mom, I'm a woman. Tom and I are getting married after school.

BELLE: *(She looks at SANDY, then)* He'll walk out on you. They all do. That's how men are. And he's no different.

SANDY: Yes he is.

BELLE: No he's not. They're all the same. He'll walk out on you. Just like all men do.

SANDY: All men? You mean *your* men.

BELLE: All men. And besides . . . you're . . .

SANDY: Yes . . . ? I'm what?

BELLE: *(Looks at her)* You're . . . naive. *(Looks away.)* You could get hurt.

SANDY: Hurt? You want to talk about hurt? Mom, you may still think I'm your little baby, but I've been hurt before. Mostly by you trying to keep me from *getting hurt.*

BELLE: I only did what I thought was best. I did what I thought was best for you.

SANDY: You used to frighten me.

BELLE: How did I frighten you?

SANDY: By saying everything was so dangerous.

BELLE: Well, I didn't want to take a chance on you getting hurt. I'm sorry if I frightened you, if I hurt you, but I did what I thought was best.

SANDY: Best for who? For me or for you?

BELLE: *(After a second of thought)* You.

SANDY: You were just overprotecting me.

BELLE: Protecting you. That's what mothers do. It's their job.

SANDY: You're overprotecting me. You always did that. Even before I left for college.

BELLE: I just wanted to protect you.

SANDY: Stop protecting me. Just be my mother. Just love me. Even when I wanted to go to my high school prom with Jerry, you became such a problem, he said forget it.

BELLE: I guess he didn't love you very much.

SANDY: Love? Who's talking about love? We were kids. We were just friends. He just enjoyed my company. *(Thinks)* Sure, I hoped maybe it would turn into something more than friendship, but you had him so intimidated, he was afraid if I came home with hiccups, you'd have him thrown into prison or something.

BELLE: I never said anything like that to him.

SANDY: Mom, you have no idea how much you said.

BELLE: I never said a thing.

SANDY: Maybe not in words, but in other ways. And not just to my friends, but to me too.

BELLE: What did I say? Tell me. What?

SANDY: **Forget it. OK?** *(Picks up photo album and begins paging through it.)* **Look at these pictures.** *(BELLE walks over and looks down at them.)* **Here I am in my prom dress.**

BELLE: **That wasn't your color.**

SANDY: **Thanks, Mom.**

BELLE: **Well, it wasn't your color.**

SANDY: *(Turning to another page)* **Look at this.**

BELLE: *(With disdain)* **That car.**

SANDY: **And my first set of hand controls.**

BELLE: **I never liked them. They never seemed safe to me.**

SANDY: **I never cared. All I cared about was getting my wheels.**

BELLE: **And speeding tickets.**

SANDY: *(Paging through photo album)* **Yep. I got a few of those.**

BELLE: **More than a few.** *(Smiling, pointing to picture)* **Look. There's your old wheelchair when it was new. The one I picked out for you.**

SANDY: *(Not happy looking at it)* **Yeah. I saw it. I like my new one.**

BELLE: **I guess you do. You picked it out.**

SANDY: **That's right.**

BELLE: *(Looking at another picture, frowns)* **Oh, there's that terrible girl. I never could stand her. What was her name?**

SANDY: *(Smiling)* **Jane. Good old Jane.**

BELLE: **I hated her.**

SANDY: **I liked her.**

BELLE: **I could never take her. I was glad when she moved away.**

SANDY: **I still miss her. She used to treat me like one of the gang. We'd go everywhere.**

BELLE: **She used to push you too fast. I always had to yell at her to slow down.**

SANDY: **I remember. She was great.**

BELLE: **Dangerous.**

SANDY: *(Smiling)* **Yeah. You should have seen us at the hill down at the park.**

BELLE: I knew it! I just knew it! You could have been killed.

SANDY: Relax, Mom.

BELLE: I just knew you were racing down that hill.

SANDY: Jane and I used to have a ball zooming down that monster. She'd hop on the back of my chair and down we'd go.

BELLE: You could have been killed.

SANDY: *(Laughing)* It was great. Jane was great.

BELLE: I never liked her.

SANDY: I know. I remember when Jane wanted me to come to her slumber party, you weren't too happy.

BELLE: I knew what that girl was up to. Boys.

SANDY: *(Smiling)* Right. Boys. Good old Jane.

BELLE: Bad old Jane. Lord knows what she's doing now.

SANDY: I wonder. We lost touch after she moved away. Jane wasn't into letter writing.

BELLE: I don't think she could write. She skipped school so often.

SANDY: *(Turning a page)* Look at Jerry. He was cute.

BELLE: Him? He was covered with acne.

SANDY: I thought he was a great guy. We used to talk on the phone for hours. I know he liked me.

BELLE: But didn't marry you.

SANDY: Mom, we were only fifteen or sixteen.

BELLE: You know what I mean. He talked to you on the phone for hours, but dated girls who could . . . dance.

SANDY: I know. You're right there. Still, he did ask me to the prom.

BELLE: I never liked him.

SANDY: You never liked any boys I liked. None of them. You'd find fault with them even before their Clearasil™ wore off. *(She puts the photo album back on the coffee table as BELLE looks away.)* You were always afraid. You never trusted my opinion, or taste in guys.

BELLE: I certainly did not. And I was never afraid.

SANDY: Look, Mom, all I know is that you were always afraid
for me. Even when I wanted to drive, all I got from you
was, "It's dangerous. You'll get into an accident."

BELLE: You might.

SANDY: *Sooo.*

BELLE: *(Annoyed)* So? You could be killed!

SANDY: I'd rather take that chance than sit around here
worrying about it.

BELLE: Well . . . it's dangerous.

SANDY: To you me crossing the street is dangerous.

BELLE: I just don't want you to get hurt. I love you.

SANDY: I know you love me, but your lack of trust in me —
in my abilities — really hurts me. You know, I don't just
want your love. I want your trust and respect too, Mom.

BELLE: I just don't want you to get hurt. I worry about you.

SANDY: I wish you'd stop doing that.

BELLE: You do? I see.

SANDY: Look. Just stop worrying about me. OK?

BELLE: *(Folding her arms)* Whatever you say.

SANDY: Look, Mom, please just stop. OK? Stop interfering in
my life.

BELLE: Sure. I'm sorry. Anything you want. What I'd like to
know is why you even bothered to come home.

SANDY: *(Silent, thinks as she rolls to edge of stage as BELLE walks
to opposite side of stage. There is a lot of distance between them.)*
Maybe to smell your cooking bacon and eggs in the
morning. Maybe I just needed to come home again. It's
like I left something here. Something. A part of me maybe.
I can't quite put my finger on it. But I know whatever it
is, it's here somewhere. *(She thinks.)* Then again, maybe
it's not here at all. Maybe it's in here. *(Lays her hand over
her heart.)* I used to think it was outside me, somewhere
else. This house, you, school, teachers, men. Anywhere,
but *(Lays her hand on her heart)* here. It was like everyone
knew more than I did. They knew where it was. Me? No.

It was like I had this little secret. This little secret I kept inside of me.

BELLE: What secret?

SANDY: I didn't tell you? *(Pauses, BELLE shakes her head no.)* Well, it was a secret. What was it? It was this feeling. Like everyone was so perfect. You know what I mean? Everyone had a perfect life. And perfectly color-coordinated clothes they looked perfectly wonderful in. They all looked perfect in their life, in this life. *(A brief pause.)* They all knew exactly how to talk, exactly how to walk, exactly how to smile — exactly how to do everything. How to dress, how to study, how to get good grades, how to get a good job, how to get guys. My friends thought I knew all that stuff, but I didn't. I figured *they* did. They were all so great at everything. But they weren't really, and neither was I. We were *all* confused. So I read everything I could find on life, love, friendship, body image. I, too, wanted to be perfect. Hey, why not? *(She shrugs.)* Don't ask me. It was like it was against Newton's third law or thermodynamics or something for me to be perfect. So I buried myself in books, in school — in that great search for truth, justice and the proverbial answer to that proverbial, eternal question. The question was, *what* was the question? *(Thinks, then)* You know what my problem was? I was watching too much TV and reading too many of those new wave fashion magazines. I had mistakenly come to the conclusion that I was not thin enough, not tall enough, not rich enough, and not good enough. Then all of a sudden one day it hit me. Wham! I am me and if no one likes me the way I am, too bad. I'm perfect the way I am. And I refuse to cater to anyone, to anyone's image or to anyone's idea of what I should be. No more would TV, the media, or you, Mom, tell me who I was. I would be me — take me or leave me. So here I am. I'm home, Mom. Home.

BELLE: Well, you just can't come home again.

SANDY: So says Thomas Wolfe and my mother.

BELLE: What?

SANDY: Nothing. I was just remembering something I read in school.

BELLE: That's another thing. Just because you're going to college, you think you know more than me. Well, baby, I've had more experience than you'll ever have. You don't know anything.

SANDY: Thanks, Mom. Thanks for the encouragement. You certainly know how to build up a person's self-confidence.

BELLE: *(Walks over to SANDY)* It's a cruel world out there! It's not like college. That's not the real world.

SANDY: Mom, I've been living in the real world all my life. I know what I'm up against. And I have to live in this world. I know it won't be easy out there. But what choice do I have?

BELLE: You have a choice of coming home.

SANDY: That's just what FDR's mother said to him after he contracted polio. Come home. You'll never amount to anything. She wanted to protect him.

BELLE: And so do I.

SANDY: Mom, you want to smother me.

BELLE: Only with love.

SANDY: That's not love. That's fear.

BELLE: What fear?

SANDY: That's what I can't quite figure out.

BELLE: Can't figure out what? You're a college girl. I thought you knew everything. What don't you know?

SANDY: If you're afraid of me getting hurt, or if you're afraid of being left all alone.

BELLE: I told you I have my friends.

SANDY: That's not what I hear.

BELLE: What are you talking about?

SANDY: I heard from Father O'Conner that ever since I went away to college, you started drifting away from the church, your bridge club and your volunteer work. *(Thinks)* Maybe that's why I came home. *(Thinks, then mumbles.)* Great. Just great.

BELLE: Great?

SANDY: You did it to me again.

BELLE: I don't understand you. What did I do?

SANDY: *(She shakes her head, realizing what is happening.)* I don't believe it.

BELLE: What don't you believe?

SANDY: That I let you do it to me again. *(Shakes her head in disgust.)* I don't believe it. I don't believe it. You've done it to me again.

BELLE: Done what? What have I done? What have I ever done to you — but loved you? What? What have I done?

SANDY: You've manipulated me into doing just what you wanted. *(Throws her hands up.)* What a jerk. What a dummy I am.

BELLE: Why? Because you loved your mother? Because you were worried about me and came home?

SANDY: No, Mom. Because I let you do it to me even now. Even after all these years away at college. I haven't learned a thing. Not a thing.

BELLE: I don't get it. I don't understand what you're talking about.

SANDY: *(SANDY gets her coat and puts it on.)* I do. God, I do.

BELLE: What are you doing? What are you talking about? Sandy? Baby? Where are you going?

SANDY: I'm going back to school.

BELLE: You mean you're running away from me.

SANDY: I have to go!

BELLE: What about me?

SANDY: Mom, now it's your turn to break down a few barriers. *(Almost in tears)* I love you, Mom. I'll always love you. I love you for being there when I needed you. For picking me up when I fell down. For all the good things you've done for me. But now it's my turn to pick myself up. And it's your turn to let me. If you really love me, you'll come visit me at school. I'm sorry. But I'm leaving, **Mom. I'm leaving!** *(SANDY exits as fast as she can, in tears.)*

BELLE: Sandy! Sandy! *(After a tiny pause)* **Button up your coat! It's cold out there!** *(Curtain falls as BELLE sits alone in old wheelchair.)*

ORDER FORM

MERIWETHER PUBLISHING LTD.
P.O. BOX 7710
COLORADO SPRINGS, CO 80933
TELEPHONE: (719) 594-4422

Please send me the following books:

_____**On Stage! Short Plays for Acting**
Students #TT-B165   **$9.95**
by Robert Mauro
24 short one-act plays for acting practice

_____**TV Scenes for Actors #TT-B137**   **$14.95**
by Sigmund A. Stoler
Selected short scenes from the Golden Age of TV Drama

_____**Encore! More Winning Monologs for Young**   **$7.95**
Actors #TT-B144
by Peg Kehret
More honest-to-life monologs for young actors

_____**Winning Monologs for Young Actors #TT-B127**   **$7.95**
by Peg Kehret
Honest-to-life monologs for young actors

_____**Two Character Plays for Student Actors #TT-B174**   **$7.95**
by Robert Mauro
A collection of 15 one-act plays

_____**Original Audition Scenes for Actors #TT-B129**   **$9.95**
by Garry Michael Kluger
A book of professional-level dialogs and monologs

_____**57 Original Auditions for Actors #TT-B181**   **$6.95**
by Eddie Lawrence
A workbook of monologs for actors

I understand that I may return any book
for a full refund if not satisfied.

NAME: _____

ORGANIZATION NAME: _____

ADDRESS: _____

CITY: _____STATE: _____ZIP: _____

PHONE: _____

☐ **Check Enclosed**
☐ **Visa or Master Card #**_____

Signature: _____
(required for Visa/Mastercard orders)

COLORADO RESIDENTS: Please add 3% sales tax.
SHIPPING: Include $1.50 for the first book and 50¢ for each additional book ordered.

☐ *Please send me a copy of your complete catalog of books or plays.*

10-90